The Salesforce Business An   Handbook

Proven business analysis techniques and processes for
a superior user experience and adoption

Srini Munagavalasa

BIRMINGHAM—MUMBAI

The Salesforce Business Analyst Handbook

Group Product Manager: Alok Dhuri
Publishing Product Manager: Akshay Dani
Senior Editor: Rohit Singh
Technical Editor: Jubit Pincy
Copy Editor: Safis Editing
Project Coordinator: Deeksha Thakkar
Proofreader: Safis Editing
Indexer: Sejal Dsilva
Production Designer: Shyam Sundar Korumilli
Business Development Executive: Uzma Sheerin
Marketing Coordinators: Deepak Kumar and Rayyan Khan

First published: October 2022

Production reference: 1211022

Published by Packt Publishing Ltd.
Livery Place
35 Livery Street
Birmingham
B3 2PB, UK.

ISBN 978-1-80181-342-6

www.packt.com

Contributors

About the author

Srini Munagavalasa has more than 20 years of global IT experience in Salesforce CRM and PRM, SAP CRM, and HR. He has a passion for learning about new and emerging technologies and products and prototyping and implementing solutions resulting in customer satisfaction and business benefits. He has authored 10+ articles on CRM, HR, and project management with **Wellesley Information Services (WIS)**. He has also presented papers at Salesforce Dreamforce and SAP Sapphire/ASUG. He is currently working as a VP at Salesforce COE at MUFG Americas. He has a bachelor's degree in metallurgical engineering and holds a post-graduate diploma in operations management. He has worked with renowned companies such as CA Tech, IBM, The Walt Disney Company, and PwC.

I would like to thank my wife, Sunanda, and my children, Sravan and Sai, for all their support and encouragement; my Packt team, for their guidance and keeping me on track; and my reviewers, for providing valuable feedback.

Finally, thanks to my family members, friends, and all my colleagues at work, who helped me learn and grow from my experiences.

About the reviewers

Jarod McCarty has 15 years of experience in the manufacturing and construction industry, 5 years of which have involved a Salesforce business analyst role.

Jarod lives with his wife and four kids in Fort Worth, TX, where he enjoys spending time with his family, spending time outdoors, and, of course, learning more about tech and Salesforce.

Andrew Nixon is a certified Salesforce application architect with over 20 years of experience in software delivery. He has a deep appreciation of all software life cycle management aspects, having progressed through support, business analyst, and program management roles delivering tier 1 ERPs and CRMs for global organizations.

In 2016, he took the decision to focus solely on Salesforce and now heads a Salesforce Centre of Excellence managing an enterprise-wide Salesforce instance.

Andrew is passionate about learning, sharing knowledge, mentoring, and upskilling his teams. In his spare time, he also volunteers as a Salesforce administrator for non-profit organizations.

Table of Contents

3

Prioritizing Requirements   33

4

Process Flows – "As-Is" versus "To-Be"   47

5

Business Requirements Document   61

Part 2: Design, Development, and Testing – Iterative Cycles with Prototypes and Conference Room Pilots

6

Solution Design and Functional Document   75

7

Demonstrate Functionality Using Prototypes   89

8

Exploring Conference Room Pilots   103

9

Technical and Quality Testing   117

10

Requirements Traceability Matrix   131

Part 3: End User Testing, Communication, Training, and Support

11

User Acceptance Testing   141

12

Communication and Knowledge Management   155

13

End User Training   165

14

Post Go-Live Support / User Forums   177

Assessments   193

Index   201

Other Books You May Enjoy   214

Preface

I have covered business analysis activities for every phase of many projects in my 20+ years of experience working on many successful global implementations. I have seen many project phases being negatively impacted by a lack of proper business analysis activities. It starts with understanding what your business users' needs are, and they are not always in black and white. This book addresses what your users' true needs are and how you, as a business analyst, can untangle and read their minds to understand the true essence of their needs and the benefits they provide to your organization. You'll get to learn various methods, tools, and techniques to help you with the analysis process. The most critical and significant activity of any project is to be able to understand what the business needs are, and if we cannot do this, it does not matter what kind of hi-fi solution your project team provides. Your project will be another artifact sitting on the shelf, dusty.

This book will help you understand various techniques to document value-added business requirements; translate these requirements into viable and acceptable solutions; verify and validate the developed and tested solutions; help end users understand how to use the new features and functions; and be a trusted advisor in supporting your end users on their journey to achieve amazing user adoption.

For projects to be successful, you do not need magic. All you need is for your team to understand business analysis processes, tools, and techniques. The chapters in this book will help guide you through business analysis activities in all project phases.

Who this book is for

This book is for intermediate- to senior-level business analysts with a basic understanding of Salesforce CRM software or any CRM technology who want to learn proven business analysis techniques to set their business up for success.

What this book covers

Chapter 1, *Identifying Requirements*, discusses the role of a business analyst and different types of software requirements. You will learn how to explore common sources to look for things that help spot and identify business requirements.

Chapter 2, *Elicitation and Document Requirements*, discusses various methods to draw out the business needs and wants from various sources. This enables you to extract sufficient information to understand users' expressed and unexpressed business needs and formalize and document them as detailed requirements.

Chapter 3, Prioritizing Requirements, covers the process and techniques of requirement prioritization, helping you understand the dependencies between various requirements and prioritize dependencies in the right order without creating gaps in the requirements flow.

Chapter 4, Process Flows – "As-is" versus "To-be", helps you understand the importance of business process flows. We will discuss how to develop and understand current and future process flows. We will see how we can identify any gaps that can be addressed and opportunities to automate the functionality.

Chapter 5, Business Requirements Document, reviews different types of requirements and the level of detail to be captured for each of these types of requirements for better understanding by all team members. We will discuss and understand the importance of documenting key attributes of a business requirement document.

Chapter 6, Solution Design and Functional Document, covers different ways to identify functional and non-functional requirements using process flows. We will cover aspects that can make the designed solution flexible, maintainable, and scalable. We will also cover transitional requirements and the critical part they play in making your projects successful.

Chapter 7, Demonstrate Functionality Using Prototypes, covers ways to demonstrate functionality by translating functional specifications into a visual working model using different techniques and tools. You will learn ways to help team members see a visual of the requirement and provide an opportunity to ideate, collaborate, and obtain feedback iteratively.

Chapter 8, Exploring Conference Room Pilots, discusses ways to collaborate and showcase prototypes to a wider audience. We will see how conference room pilots can help us progress from individual requirements to proposed design solutions in the right direction. We will also discuss how various team members can benefit and add value to other project phases.

Chapter 9, Technical and Quality Testing, reviews and shows how testing helps us with exploring the system to verify, validate, and confirm that the system functionality developed works as intended. We will explore and see what tools, traits, and skills make effective testing. We will explore various testing approaches, testing phases, and testing types.

Chapter 10, Requirements Traceability Matrix, helps you understand the importance of the relationships between requirements and various project artifacts and how they help us establish traceability. We will explore how this helps us in identifying and in bridging any elusive gaps. We will also see how to link requirements to project deliverables, ensuring that we have complete test coverage.

Chapter 11, User Acceptance Testing, shows how user acceptance plays a crucial role in a successful Go-Live. We will discuss how to work with business users and help them test real-life business scenarios and get feedback on usability. We will also discuss how to plan and execute user acceptance testing in a structured way that can reduce post-production issues and save the organization's time and resources.

Chapter 12, Communication and Knowledge Management, discusses aspects of communication and knowledge management, especially focused on end users. We will explore various options to make sure we provide timely and appropriate communication. You will learn how to tailor knowledge management artifacts related to the usage of the functions of the new systems.

Chapter 13, End User Training, discusses the important role end user training plays in the successful adoption of the system functionality by end users. We will see how to train and prepare users so that they can understand the core system functionality, integrations, and business process flows.

Chapter 14, Post-Go-Live Support / User Forums, covers details on why post-go-live support is so critical for users to adjust to the system's new functionality. We will learn to plan and facilitate user forums with end users that help establish continued collaboration. We will see what makes you a trusted advisor to your users and help continuously improve the system and its usage.

Download the color images

We also provide a PDF file that has color images of the screenshots and diagrams used in this book. You can download it here: `https://packt.link/WeXkm`.

Conventions used

There are a number of text conventions used throughout this book.

Bold: Indicates a new term, an important word, or words that you see onscreen. For instance, words in menus or dialog boxes appear in **bold**. Here is an example: "Select **System info** from the **Administration** panel."

> **Tips or important notes**
> Appear like this.

Get in touch

Feedback from our readers is always welcome.

General feedback: If you have questions about any aspect of this book, email us at `customercare@packtpub.com` and mention the book title in the subject of your message.

Errata: Although we have taken every care to ensure the accuracy of our content, mistakes do happen. If you have found a mistake in this book, we would be grateful if you would report this to us. Please visit `www.packtpub.com/support/errata` and fill in the form.

Piracy: If you come across any illegal copies of our works in any form on the internet, we would be grateful if you would provide us with the location address or website name. Please contact us at `copyright@packt.com` with a link to the material.

If you are interested in becoming an author: If there is a topic that you have expertise in and you are interested in either writing or contributing to a book, please visit `authors.packtpub.com`.

Share Your Thoughts

Once you've read *The Salesforce Business Analyst Handbook*, we'd love to hear your thoughts! Scan the QR code below to go straight to the Amazon review page for this book and share your feedback.

https://packt.link/r/1-801-81342-6

Your review is important to us and the tech community and will help us make sure we're delivering excellent quality content.

Download a free PDF copy of this book

Thanks for purchasing this book!

Do you like to read on the go but are unable to carry your print books everywhere? Is your eBook purchase not compatible with the device of your choice?

Don't worry, now with every Packt book you get a DRM-free PDF version of that book at no cost.

Read anywhere, any place, on any device. Search, copy, and paste code from your favorite technical books directly into your application.

The perks don't stop there, you can get exclusive access to discounts, newsletters, and great free content in your inbox daily

Follow these simple steps to get the benefits:

1. Scan the QR code or visit the link below

https://packt.link/free-ebook/9781801813426

2. Submit your proof of purchase
3. That's it! We'll send your free PDF and other benefits to your email directly

Part 1:
Planning and Analysis – BRD/ Prioritized Product Backlog

In this part, you will learn about planning and analysis activities, starting with ways to identify the right sources of requirements and use elicitation techniques to understand business needs by engaging the right stakeholders. You will learn how to utilize tacit business analysis and Salesforce system analysis skills to rank and stack all requirements, and communicate and get buy-in from all stakeholders. Finally, you will document all your prioritized requirements in a business requirement document artifact. You will also learn how to create a roadmap to deliver a set of high-level requirements.

We will address some of the key challenges faced during this phase:

- Not being able to identify the right requirements, resulting in delivering unnecessary nice-to-have features without adding any business value

- Due to a lack of requirements or product backlog prioritization, projects not delivering the right solutions as requirements are accepted on a first-come, first-served basis, or the loudest voice gets prioritized

- Going all in rather than defining a clear Salesforce roadmap

- Not assessing the dependencies and integration impacts on concurrent Salesforce projects

- No clear understanding of what the current state process looks like or what the future proposed state process should be

The following chapters will be covered under this part:

- *Chapter 1, Identifying Requirements*
- *Chapter 2, Elicitation and Document Requirements*
- *Chapter 3, Prioritizing Requirements*
- *Chapter 4, Process Flows – "As-Is" versus "To-Be"*
- *Chapter 5, Business Requirements Document*

1

Identifying Requirements

In this chapter, we will discuss the role of a Business Analyst and different types of software requirements. Then, we will review some important factors that will help gain project sponsors' confidence and trust. Finally, we will explore common sources to look out for that help us spot and identify business requirements. We will also touch upon, at a high level, some business analysis lingo that you should be aware of to be able to facilitate business analysis activities. Remember, we wish to identify requirements at a very high level. We will do a deep dive into understanding requirements in more detail and from different perspectives during the elicitation phase, which will be covered in the next chapter.

In this chapter, we will cover the following topics:

- The role of business analysis in identifying requirement sources
- Securing support from the project sponsor
- Common sources where you can identify business requirements
- Real-life scenarios with examples
- Practical tips for success

By the end of this chapter, you will have a good idea of where and how to find requirements that will help you with requirements gathering. You'll also know what you should do to understand current processes and observe the inefficiencies, roadblocks, and opportunities surrounding them.

The role of business analysis in identifying requirement sources

Before we get into details of the business analysis role, let's quickly review what some common terms mean, which will be helpful in our upcoming discussions:

- **Business analysis**: Business analysis is a practice that involves understanding the current capabilities and needs of the business users, identifying gaps in the current processes, and enabling desired future capabilities to derive efficiencies, competitive advantage, and business benefits.

- **Business Analyst**: A Business Analyst is someone who practices business analysis while utilizing various tools, techniques, and resources. The goal is to help businesses move from their current state to a desired future state by understanding business needs, pain points, opportunities and gaps in processes, and providing robust, efficient, and effective solutions that are simple and usable.

- **Customer Relationship Management (CRM)**: CRM is the practice of helping customers manage sales, service, and marketing processes effectively and efficiently so that they can grow their business and provide excellent customer service.

- **Salesforce**: Salesforce is a cloud-based CRM technology platform that helps organizations serve their customers with CRM functionality.

With this basic understanding, let's discuss business analysis in detail.

Business analysis work starts with planning – there is no one cookie-cutter approach that works for every project. Business Analysts need to know and understand the context and characteristics of the project to ensure that the planning activities are scoped accordingly. Prior planning and spending time on identifying the user requirement sources will lead to a better understanding of the scope of business analysis work, stakeholders' expectations, and the amount of analysis work that needs to be done in subsequent phases of the project. We need to create a well-thought-out business analysis roadmap so that the analysis process is effective and successful.

As a Business Analyst, the first and foremost task to focus on is identifying business needs. Business needs are gaps between the current state of a business and its expected goals. Business needs analysis is also referred to as gap analysis – the current "as-is" state versus the desired "to-be" state. Needs are the basic drivers of change. By understanding needs, the Business Analyst can document requirements. This activity happens during the project planning or pre-project phase. As an analyst, you will use this data as a starting point for requirement gathering and elicitation or to create a business plan and provide findings for management decision-making.

Before you get into the requirements, you need to plan and identify where you can get the business needs and requirements. What are the good quality sources and where can you find them? These can be from stakeholders, documents, existing processes, observations, interviews, and so on.

I have worked on multiple global projects where the projects started at different stages. Most of the time, the majority of the functions that are needed are on existing systems – enhancing or adding more capabilities. I got the opportunity to work on a few projects where, as a Business Analyst, it was me who would guide the business, identify requirements, tools, and systems, and provide a system that the business can benefit from and value. This is very stressful as well as rewarding when you have to guide stakeholders and help them understand their requirements and needs. I will touch upon various examples along the way that may benefit you.

There are three possible business requirement scenarios that I would like to cover:

- The system is already in use and business users would like to request enhancements. Here, you must add additional features to existing functionality. This can be your minor enhancement release or a production support item such as a defect or maintenance item.

- The system is already in use and business users would like new functionality. This can be a brand-new functionality and addressed via a project.

- You must add new capabilities to address usability and adoption issues. This can be a complex requirement where multiple stakeholders are involved.

Based on these scenarios, let's explore our analysis process. Examples for each of these scenarios have been provided with screenshots in the *Real-life scenarios with examples* section.

Project teams and IT teams most often blame the business users, stating that they do not know what they want. That is the very reason why we have Project Managers, Business Analysts, IT teams, QA teams, training teams, and so on. Business users do not need to know what they want. It is up to the project team, especially the Business Analyst, to identify the right stakeholders, pull ideas out of users, and get agreement from everyone.

Stakeholders, even though they know the problems in most cases, do not know how to articulate their needs. On the other hand, few users can articulate, anticipate, and lay out their needs, wants, and desires, and pretty much want everything their way. You need to be cognizant of both and watchful for the latter.

In reality, only a few requirements are documented in some form. Most of them reside in the heads of stakeholders, end users, and process flows that are yet to be understood and developed.

For a project to be successful, understanding and documenting requirements accurately is one of the key success factors. Failure to understand and capture requirements accurately will lead to project delays, false expectations, broken promises, blame games, and stressful situations. So, let's focus on learning, understanding, discovering, and getting the right requirements by focusing on extracting the ideas, issues wants, and needs of the users.

> **Note**
> I will be covering real-life practical scenarios – successes as well as failures and lessons learned. We will use many existing Business Analyst tools and techniques. As needed, I will explain them at a very high level. I will not be providing definitions or procedures; instead, I will explain the scenarios with practical examples based on my experience.

Let's delve into what it takes to identify business needs and wants. Our ultimate end goal here is to identify a set of requirements that are consistent, non-redundant, and complete. In this chapter, we shall concentrate only on the extent of learning problems and/or opportunities to sufficiently understand the situation and not perform a complete requirement analysis, which shall be explained in future chapters. Ensure that you're not subjective and judgmental; you are here to understand business needs, not design solutions. As Business Analysts, we must make every effort to understand business needs and wants, how they align with the vision/strategy, and how this enables us to achieve our strategic end goal.

As Business Analysts, we need to get as much information as possible by exploring all possible avenues and areas. You need to know what information you must get and where to find that information. For that, we need to ask six (**5Ws + 1H** – Who, What, When, Where, Why, and How) questions iteratively to completely understand the full scope and intent of the business needs. When asking these questions, you should know the rationale for every question and be able to explain to stakeholders why that question is relevant.

By understanding different types of requirements, you will be able to manage the requirements process effectively at all project stages. Remind yourself that we are here to gather information to identify the real problem or opportunity and not to provide our opinions or solutions.

Types of requirements

There are four main types of requirements, as listed here:

- **Business requirements**: An example of this is if you are implementing a new system or functionality. These requirements are the most complex to understand, as there are too many unknowns. These requirements describe the high-level functionality that the business needs.

- **Stakeholder requirements**: Also called user requirements, these are features and functions that the users need and specify how they interact with the system. Getting to know the stakeholders' needs and wants is critical because, often, they may not be able to articulate them clearly. This is very critical as stakeholder requirements are later translated into system requirements. Any flaws here get amplified at later stages and result in rework.

- **System requirements**: These requirements describe the characteristics of the solution. There are two types of system requirements:

  - **Functional**: Describes a specific set of capabilities

  - **Non-functional**: Describes the characteristics

- **Transition requirements**: These are transient requirements and are needed for a short period. Make sure that you discuss and get details around transition requirements. They are essential and critical to project success.

The most notable requirement is data migration. In the process of ETL, data may be rendered useless if data migration is not done diligently. I have seen many instances in projects, including the one I worked on a few years ago, where, after converting HR data, the team was unable to run the payroll on time. You know what's going to happen if employees are not paid on time.

Knowing and understanding different requirement types and establishing goals and timelines for identifying requirements will help pave the foundation for the next step of our business analysis. Here, we are trying to understand the current state and the desired future state. Analyzing business needs and wants will help us provide the right solution or address the right problem during our design phase.

In the past 15 years, I have worked on multiple Salesforce implementations: Sales Cloud, Service Cloud, and Partner Relationship Management. I employed more than one method to get to know and understand business needs. It all depends on your implementation methodology, people, culture, IT team maturity, and so on, and you need to tailor and use a combination of the methods discussed in the *Common sources where you can identify business requirements* section, later in this chapter.

Securing support from the project sponsor

Securing support from a project sponsor is another important factor for any project to succeed. The business analysis process and the Business Analyst play a vital role in securing confidence and trust with the project sponsors. Business analysis involves defining the requirements, designing the solution, communicating, validating the solution, and training activities so that they are well positioned to access and identify project impacts. They can act as the eyes and ears of the project sponsor. The project sponsor often depends on project managers and Business Analysts for all key decision-making. Just like gaining confidence and trust from **subject matter experts** (**SMEs**), project team members, and super users, we have to gain the project sponsor's confidence and trust too. One of the most important activities is to keep the sponsor in the loop at all times.

As a Business Analyst, you can gain project sponsors' trust and confidence by assisting them with information and the decision-making process. This is possible through good planning and communication. Let's outline what you should be doing to help the sponsor:

- Present information accurately and concisely at the appropriate level.

- Issues are bound to arise, so be prepared with the information and facts to facilitate smooth decision-making.

- At each stage of the project, provide a summary of the business analysis work while highlighting achievements and any risks.

- As a key resource, be prepared and provide recommendations with pros and cons.

- Be truthful, transparent, and courageous to deliver unpleasant information. Be able to say "No."

Gaining confidence and trust will help Business Analysts navigate business analysis work smoothly, efficiently, and productively. This will help the project team and you, as a Business Analyst, in areas such as the following:

- Resources availability for SMEs and other project resources

- Timely decision making

- Provide direction – define the scope, prioritize requirements, and so on

- Influence escalations, resolve conflicts, and motivate

Common sources where you can identify business requirements

Now that we understand how to identify requirements and why it is important for a business, let's review the various sources where we can gather these requirements.

Document analysis

Document analysis involves getting your hands on any relevant documentation: scope documents, project initiation requests, business plans, knowledge transfer artifacts, manuals, presentations, minutes of past meetings, user guides, and so on.

Identify key stakeholders

Who shall be impacted by the change directly or indirectly? You can start with a business sponsor and a program manager. Find out the scope and range of the project implementation in terms of various **Business Units (BUs)**.

Navigate the organization

Get to know SMEs, data captains, planning team members who focus on analytics and management dashboards, and a few enthusiastic end users.

Current system usage

Find out how current systems are used to perform their job and how they are integrated into other systems in the company.

This is a great opportunity for you to observe and find opportunities to enhance and simplify the processes and save time and frustration.

An example would be users struggling to access the system due to login issues (incorrect password or system lockout due to too many incorrect password attempts). This can be easily addressed via enabling **Single Sign-On** (**SSO**), which is available out of the box for almost all cloud applications. With SSO, users need to click on one bookmarked URL to access an application.

Identify the key end user

Users who are passionate about the change and who are direct beneficiaries understand existing work practices and existing unaddressed problems. I listed them separately as they are not identified as part of the project stakeholders. They can be your level 1 support or call center representative.

Plan brainstorming sessions by facilitating the conversation and allowing key participants to openly debate and speak out. Take notes and make sure that you let the conversation flow freely; your job is to facilitate the conversation and ask questions as appropriate.

Needs decomposition

Try to get as much information from whatever source possible via decomposition, breaking down needs into smaller needs until they can no longer be decomposed. This way, we are breaking down a complex requirement into multiple small and simplified individual components of the needs.

Get a system walkthrough

Understand firsthand how end users normally use the system regularly. Be an observer and let the user navigate and walk through their process in the system end to end. This user journey helps you understand and identify missed elements and any usability requirements.

Active participation

Listen attentively and actively, acknowledge, ask questions, and rephrase what you heard and understood. This is to ensure an accurate understanding of what has been communicated is agreed by both ends. Also, avoid judging what you heard so that information flows freely. Focus on business needs and do not get into designing the solution.

Most often, the stakeholder assumes that the Business Analyst already knows or is aware of the business needs and provides high-level information only. Business Analysts need to make sure that information is provided in enough detail.

Let the participants debate and let them vent their frustration. You get facts and truth from this kind of conversation and are able to grasp stakeholders' perspectives of business needs.

Different stakeholders may have different perspectives; it is your job to explore them and resolve any conflicts.

Make sure you keep the discussion aligned to the agenda and manage it so that it doesn't get out of control.

Existing systems

Find ways to get access to current systems and be able to run some key reports and dashboards. This will help you identify and get reports and stats on end users who use the system.

During one of my first implementations, I was able to run a few reports and find out who the power users were. I ran stats and saw why usage dropped from quarter to quarter (or over a period). By doing this, along with the data and facts I had gathered, I was well prepared to ask the users the right questions.

Note-taking

Take notes, prepare minutes, and share them with the participants on the same day and solicit feedback. Clarify any open queries one on one with specific participants.

When taking notes, make sure that you tag the requirement type as business, stakeholder, solution, or transition. By understanding the requirement type, you can fine-tune and facilitate the conversation effectively and efficiently.

Assumptions

Avoid and eliminate all assumptions around requirements. Business needs must be verified and assumptions, if any, need to be confirmed and documented.

Meeting minutes

Prepare and share a list of simple, clear, consistent, and complete high-level requirements. This will help you provide the steps that must be taken.

Now that we have learned where and how we can identify and gather business requirements, let's learn how to implement them with some real-world examples. These will be covered in the next section.

Real-life scenarios with examples

Business needs vary from very simple to extremely complex. With the help of three different practical scenarios, I will explain the various needs and discuss how they are addressed and implemented. A strong understanding of business needs will help us in the elicitation phase.

Scenario 1

This is a simple scenario where users know what they need. It could be an existing pain point where I am looking for improvements. This case is true when users are already using the system and they can easily point out the gaps, be it defects or enhancements to the application.

For example, in Salesforce, duplicate leads, accounts, and contact records cause multiple issues down the line. These types of requirements are very straightforward. As a Salesforce-savvy Business Analyst, I can provide a quick solution. Here, I could suggest that users use the available duplicate management functionality.

By understanding the business needs, we can fulfill this requirement quickly by using existing out-of-the-box features from Salesforce. We will be able to find a quick solution for the majority of simple requirements. The key is to understand the business needs.

This is an example where elicitation is straightforward as business needs can be articulated easily and clearly.

> **Note**
> You may have to do a one-time cleanup of existing data to implement this solution.

Duplicate management functionality on the contact record

Here, we shall implement a rule where the Salesforce system will prevent users from creating duplicate contacts if the last name and email combination match.

A duplicate rule with matching criteria can be quickly implemented. Whenever any users try to create a duplicate contact, the system should prevent the user from creating one. The following screenshot shows a duplication rule being created:

Figure 1.1 – Creating a duplicate rule

In the following screenshot, I tried to create another contact with the same last name and email address. By implementing a simple duplicate rule, the system should prevent duplicate contact records:

New Contact

Contact Information

Contact Owner	SM Business Analysis	Phone	
*Name	Salutation	Home Phone	
	Mr.		
	First Name		
	Business1		
	*Last Name		
	Analyst		
Account Name	Business Analysis LLC ✕	Mobile	
Title		Other Phone	
Department	⊘ We hit a snag. ✕		
Birthdate	You can't save this record because a duplicate record already exists. To save, use different information.		business@analyst.com
Reports To	View Duplicates	stant	

⊘   Cancel   Save & New   Save

Figure 1.2 – Salesforce system preventing users from creating a duplicate contact

You can view the duplicate as shown. Here, users will be able to make any updates as needed to the existing contact record:

View Duplicates

Contact with Same Email ID and Last Name exists! Do you really want to create a Dupe record?

CONTACT (1)

Business1 Analyst
Contact

Name: Business1 Analyst
Account Name: Business Analysis LLC
Account Site:
Phone:
Email: business@analyst.com
Contact Owner Alias: SMun

Open This Contact

Figure 1.3 – Option to view the existing duplicate contact record

You can also propose a more robust solution using AppExchange packages such as Demand Tool, which is an excellent tool for keeping your data clean and relevant. This is a managed package and there is a subscription fee per user. There are many paid and free tools on AppExchange. Do your research and try them in a sandbox before deciding to use them in your production environment.

Scenario 2

Users want field attributes defaulted by the system so that they can avoid re-keying the same data again for a specific BU.

For example, the billing address that's available on the account record shall default when creating contact records for specific country users.

To illustrate this, we will look at another simple example where users can update their billing address with a company billing address. By automating this, the data quality stays accurate, current, and relevant. In Salesforce, this can be achieved via Process Builder. You can do the same with Flow Builder too. Process Builder will replace Flow Builder going forward, so it is advisable to start flows for automation:

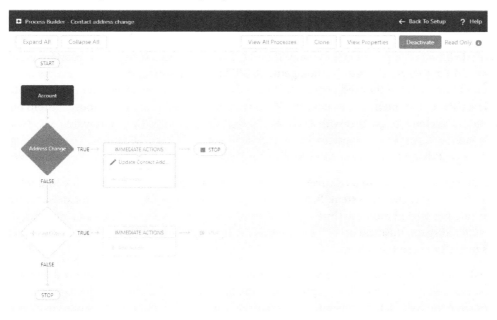

Figure 1.4 – Using Process Builder to automate address updates on the contact record

Let's look at another example. In Salesforce, the Sales team would like to see certain fields from the User record and Account record defaulted on the **Opportunity record** page. This requirement requires some level of analysis.

To simplify this, let's look at a simplified requirement. A specific BU user would like to default certain field attributes from the User record (such as Region, Country, Division, and Department) and Account record (such as Account Owner, Industry, Account Type, and Rating). The rationale for this requirement is to have information available on the same Opportunity record and also be able to create list views from the **Opportunities** tab. To simplify further, let's assume you, as a Business Analyst, socialized this with other BU stakeholders and got confirmation that they would like to have the same functionality extended to all.

You can have multiple solutions in Salesforce. Here, you can go with flows, but the simplest and easiest solution is to create a formula field. In our case, this is the preferred solution as users need data with view access; any updates that are made to user or account attributes are immediately reflected on the **Opportunity record** page.

This example helps you elicit unexpressed business needs. By observing or analyzing the ways to improve data quality, you, as a Business Analyst, shall be able to suggest the needs to business users and implement the same. Implementing these unexpressed needs helps in maintaining quality data and also reduces the time it will take the user to create data.

Scenario 3

This scenario is more complex than the others. These are instances where, in one of my previous projects when we did **Partner Relationship Management** (**PRM**) in Salesforce, the business users needed systems and functions but they did not exactly know how to explain or articulate the requirement. At a high level, the requirement was to have the PRM system migrated from an in-house custom build system to a sales cloud for partner with Account, Contact, Opportunity, Case, Campaign, Quote, and Lead Management, plus Partner Locator, Partner Onboarding, and User Onboarding. This was a hugely complex project that was delivered successfully over 3 years incrementally using agile methodology.

As an example, let me explain a relatively simple scenario. We have low adoption due to duplicate accounts and contacts in the system. Before they approached our project team, data stewards from the planning team tried multiple times to clean the data manually. But within a few months, data quality suffered again. Business users want these recurring dupe issues to be fixed as soon as possible as users may stop using the system.

After analyzing and researching internally and externally, we can identify the right product for our business. This not only enables us to capture good quality data but also enriches the data records by synchronizing the right data at a specific set frequency. This saves a lot of time, and our business can have accurate, complete, and meaningful data. We used a popular tool that is completely integrated with Salesforce. As Business Analysts, we need to be open-minded, understand business needs, and find the right solutions. In this case, rather than developing the Salesforce platform in-house, we found external tools to get the job done with minimal resources. The tool we used was an AppExchange product called D&B Hoover. This has a paid subscription managed package that is seamlessly integrated with Salesforce. Once synced up, the tool updates more than 100 account and contact attributes and adds a D&B identifier:

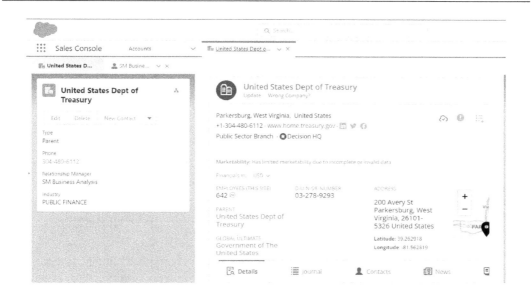

Figure 1.5 – D&B tool integrated with Salesforce on the Account Management page's layout

Since this tool is embedded seamlessly into Salesforce Account and Contact Pages, users can access this tool without the need for a separate login. In addition to customer and contact data, sales teams will be able to get innovative analytical features:

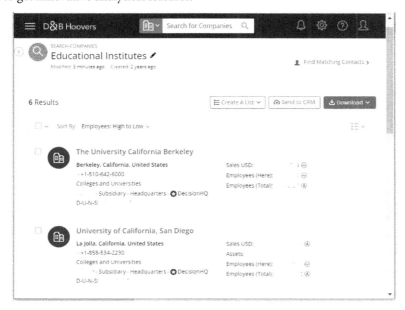

Figure 1.6 – Example where users can search for companies and sync them to Salesforce with one click

This example helps us to see that business needs are not always obvious. In this case, the business user did not even state their needs. By analyzing the root cause of low adoption, we interacted with many key stakeholders and SMEs to understand the needs. Then, we explored internal and external tools and found the one that best fits our needs. Sometimes, the end goal will help us with eliciting and drawing forth a business need that can have a positive impact on our business users.

Now, let's look at some practical tips that I found useful.

Practical tips for success

I would like to outline a few pointers that you can use when you do business analysis tasks. These are relatively simple tasks that helped me tremendously. The simplest and easy-to-do items are always overlooked. You can avoid common causes of missing out on understanding business needs by taking note of the following pointers:

- Understand the goals and objectives of the business analysis work that you plan to perform. You should be in a position to explain in simple terms why you are performing these activities.

- For any business analysis effort to be successful and to be able to identify needs, analysts need to gain trust from stakeholders. This is a long process and needs to be earned. I would encourage you to start it early.

- Get to know the stakeholders. You can get information from organizational charts or social profiles.

- Schedule meetings in advance. Make sure that you find the right time and location/medium and block time in advance.

- Provide an agenda. Prepare and communicate it a day or so before the meeting.

- Facilitate the meeting and make sure that you encourage everyone to contribute. Your job is to facilitate discussion and mediate any conflicts.

- Capture notes (assign one of your team members who is good at note-taking) and send out the minutes.

- Follow up as needed until you and the stakeholders understand and agree to high-level requirements.

- Do not get into designing solutions. Understand the business requirements. If you're savvy with Salesforce and CRM technologies, if you know a requirement is not feasible because of design constraints, say so and place it in the parking lot. Being open and honest will help build trust in the long run.

- Approach with a design-thinking mindset. Look for people and their needs before feasibility and viability. This automatically maximizes usability and user experience. Your goal should be to gain a good understanding of the complete situation and not provide options or solutions.

- Ask end users and stakeholders how their needs benefit them and their business unit. If this need is not fulfilled, do they have a workaround?

With this, we have completed this chapter on how to identify sources of requirements.

Summary

In this chapter, you learned where to find the sources of business user needs. By doing so, you learned how to get the requirements at a very high level and the key sources where you can plan to elaborate by eliciting more granular details. You also understood the key terms and ways to prepare yourself for the next stage of the requirement elicitations activity by utilizing the skills you learned in this chapter.

In the next chapter, we will discuss various ways to draw out user business needs and wants from various sources that we've identified so far. We will cover different techniques and extract information to accurately understand users' requirements.

Questions

1. Explain the difference between functional and non-functional requirements in one sentence.
2. Name a few non-functional requirements.

Further reading

- *Business Analysis Body of Knowledge (BABOK®) Guide*, by IIBA, Lightning Source Inc
- *The PMI Guide to Business Analysis*, by Au Project Management Institute
- Trailhead, by Salesforce: `https://trailhead.salesforce.com/`

2
Elicitation and Document Requirements

In the previous chapter, you did all the planning in identifying the sources from which you can elicit the business needs. In this chapter, we will discuss various methods to draw out those needs and requirements from various sources. We will dive deep into various sources and you will learn a few cool tips that you can implement during your elicitation phase. Our end goal here is to extract sufficient information to understand users' requirements.

We will also look into best practices to efficiently and effectively document these requirements. As we process elicitation iteratively, we document them right from the start and we keep refining them as we understand them more and more. Our goal here is to document all requirements – needs, wants, nice to haves, and assumptions – and come up with a solid list of all requirements that can be understood by stakeholders. Requirement elicitation is an iterative loop: you plan, prepare, conduct, and document. Elicitation is the art of discovering the real problem to be solved.

We will cover the following topics in this chapter:

- Elicitation planning
- Requirement elicitation techniques
- Requirement documentation
- The art of elicitation
- Practical tips for success

By the end of this chapter, you will understand elicitation planning, process, and techniques, and be able to produce high-quality documented requirements.

Elicitation planning

Before you start the elicitation, you need to plan and prepare. Consider the following tasks and any other tasks, and do as much research as possible so that you can maximize the outcome:

- **What information do I need to elicit?**: Make a list and always have options and alternatives.

- **Where are the sources of information?**: You already know this from the previous chapter.

- **How do I extract information from these sources?**: What techniques do we utilize?

- **What order to elicit**: You need to follow a logical order for free flow of discussion. Be flexible as the order can vary based on stakeholders and the situation.

> **Note:**
>
> For effective elicitation or, as a matter of fact, for any business meeting/discussions, do the following:
>
> - Know the players – learn about the participants
>
> - Secure commitment and set up meetings
>
> - Prepare an agenda
>
> - Facilitate meetings
>
> - Capture notes
>
> - Summarize and send out a recap

Elicitation tasks

The following are the elicitations tasks that I follow religiously. You need to plan and prepare to utilize time and resources effectively and efficiently. This means you need to spend lots of time doing your homework. In my opinion, for every 1 hour of elicitation sessions with users, be prepared to spend approximately 5 to 6 hours of pre- and post-work. Time spent on preparation pays for itself by accurately capturing true business requirements. Any incorrect requirements will result in solutions that do not meet business need:

1. **Prepare**: This step involves the following activities:

   - Your goals for the elicitation

   - Prepare the required material/artifacts

   - Identify and prepare a stakeholder list

   - Collect supporting material

   - Techniques you plan to use, and so on

2. **Conduct**: This is when you are performing the elicitation activities. You have to use a combination of tools, techniques, and styles to keep stakeholders engaged and collaborative. You can employ research, collaborative, or experimental types of elicitation. Like any good meeting, you need to structure the elicitation sessions with an introduction, the main content, a closing summary, and a follow-up.

3. **Confirm/Validate**: In this step, you are at the end of the elicitation session and summarizing business requirements. You verify with participants that the information you gather is understandable, complete, accurate, and consistent.

4. **Communicate**: Summarize meeting minutes, list out all the requirements elicited and agreed upon during the session, and capture the discussion around open items, assumptions, and gaps. This communication shall go to all stakeholders: the business as a whole, SMEs, and technical, project management, and quality assurance teams.

5. **Collaborate**: Managing stakeholder/SME collaboration is a very important activity. You can get great input from them if you can get their time and effort. Getting commitment with their busy schedules will be a challenging task. The purpose of the collaboration is to get stakeholder participation, contribution, consensus, and agreement. There will be disagreement and heated discussions, which when handled adroitly yield productive, innovative out-of-the-box thinking.

Business requirements evolve as you continue elicitations. They get refined and you will be able to extract more granular details. Time permitting, the more iterations you do, the better you get to understand the requirements, and this also helps you find gaps and identify new requirements at an early stage.

Requirement elicitation techniques

There are multiple techniques that you can use for your elicitation activity. There can be multiple factors why you may have to choose one technique over another. As a business analyst, you pick the one that meets your objectives within the given resources and constraints. We will discuss some of the techniques that I and my team utilized with great success. What techniques you use depends on many factors. I used many and some of them never worked in my project scenarios while others worked very well. What technique we use depends on the context and you need to have a complete awareness of the context in which you are doing elicitation. For example, doing an elicitation activity for an existing production system is different from the one you plan to do for a completely new implementation.

Since Salesforce CRM is a cloud-based SaaS solution, the way to gather requirements varies greatly compared to one that is an on-premise application. As an example, with cloud applications such as Salesforce, we do not need to worry about scaling the system based on data volume or user base as long as we follow Salesforce guidelines. The Salesforce SaaS platform has a governor limit that prevents the system from crashing.

In this section, we will cover the following techniques with examples. There are more techniques than those listed here, so you can use techniques that you are comfortable with and that work best for you:

- Observation
- Brainstorming
- Surveys
- Interviews / focus groups
- Conference room pilots / requirement workshops
- Prototyping
- Process model
- User stories

Let us go through each technique in greater detail so that you can get a better understanding so that you can tailor your elicitation process by using the right technique.

Observation

This technique may be the easiest one if you have good business and system knowledge. You can pretty much go to any super users and ask them to walk you through their daily process – a day in a life of their daily activities. For example, consider the service agent handling customer complaints. How they utilize the current system – navigation steps to be able to access and create cases, find customer account and contact information, the ability to find knowledge articles and link to similar issues, routing important cases to level 2 or the supervisor, and so on. By observing each step, taking notes, and asking the right questions, you will be able to understand their needs and pain points or identify opportunities to make the process simpler and better. This technique removes the communication barrier as the agent does not need to articulate their issues verbally.

Your job is to capture and take notes, ask questions, and confirm each step. Make sure to observe any gaps in the flow and ask questions to find out how they handle those gaps and the pain points around them. Do not provide or even think of designing a solution.

Brainstorming

This method helps you when you are working on completely new functionality, and no one knows exactly what they want and how they want it. You involve SMEs from business, functional, and technical teams. Brainstorming, when facilitated well, will help each individual to speak out loud and dump all their knowledge – relevant or irrelevant. This technique will help you gather a vast amount of information that can provide you with a good sense of direction. Coupled with other techniques, you can better your understanding of the requirements.

Your job here is to make sure you do the following:

- Occasionally provide them an insight with thought-provoking queries
- Encourage everyone, especially the shy ones, to speak out freely
- Encourage healthy conflict to generate ideas and manage conflict if it tends to get out of control

Surveys

A survey is another useful technique that you can use to elicit requirements in a structured manner in a short period of time.

This technique is helpful to gather information and opinions from a large number of people and from diverse groups and business units across your organization or business unit. You can also use this to validate the information that you gathered from workshops or focus groups and find agreement or disagreements. This validation task helps you in the long run with better user adoption.

Surveys are a set of questions that you can send or ask identified stakeholders, groups, subject matter experts, end users, and so on. Their responses are collected, documented, and analyzed to get knowledge about their interests or issues. Survey questions should be designed in a logical manner to ensure the needed information is obtained efficiently and effectively.

Survey techniques include the following:

- **Questionnaire**: Participants can individually answer a set of questions. This is quick but the response rate will be low and responses may be vague.
- **Interviews**: This involves asking questions 1-on-1 following up with more questions based on the responses. This technique is time-consuming but the outcome is many times better than the previous one.

To obtain good participation from respondents, you'll need to do the following:

- Define your objective so that the respondent understands why they are spending time on the survey.
- Use a wide range of question types to keep your participants engaged. Keep survey questions mixed (closed-ended, open-ended, and multiple choice). If the survey is for new functionality, open-ended responses will provide you with innovative responses.
- Tailor survey invitations and distribute them in a way that best fits the participant's needs. There are many tools you can use to plan, create, distribute, collect, summarize, and report surveys. If you use a CRM tool such as Salesforce, you can use and manage surveys from that tool.

Analyze responses by generating reports and metrics from survey responses. Based on your analysis, you will be able to identify and understand the needs. This data can be further distilled and can be used for a new level of elicitation using a different technique.

Interviews / focus groups

This is when you set up meetings with individuals or small groups. Wherever possible, it will be beneficial if interviews or focus group sessions are done in person or via live video chats. The key stakeholders that you would usually interact with are SMEs and power users such as Sales Operations or Planning teams. If conducted well, by asking the right questions, you will be able to gather a wealth of information. Remember to go to the sessions well prepared as you may not get more than a few hours. SMEs and power users mostly have a wealth of knowledge, so we need to be careful when asking questions. Make sure you understand what you are asking and elaborate as needed and ask the right and relevant questions.

I've seen many business analysis books/videos saying *keep asking questions repeatedly till you get a defined answer*. Believe me, it will not work. You need to know the business area well and, to a very good extent, understand the system too. Being knowledgeable and asking intelligent questions with supporting facts and figures will help gain their trust and they need to believe that you know what you are doing. Again, you need to use your judgment as there may be scenarios where something may sound silly, and you may not be fully conversant in a specific area. In this situation, if you know the users from before and if they trust your knowledge, you can go ahead and get clarifications, else you can note it down, do some research, and take it offline with specific users.

Wherever possible, try to record the conversation. Nowadays, it is very easy to do it on any collaboration tools such as Teams, WebEx, and Slack. This will offer you a chance to be able to replay and review the conversations/transcriptions.

The follow-up conversations need not be as formal. I prefer to take people out for a coffee or business lunch and have conversations.

Conference room pilots / requirements workshops

Conference room pilots / workshops are usually three- to four-day workshops offsite or in a conference room without any distractions and full-day sessions. In my experience, for these sessions to be effective, I recommend three sessions (for medium- to high-complexity projects). For simple enhancements or additional functionality on an existing system, a session duration of a few hours should be fine.

For my complex to medium-complexity projects, I usually schedule three sessions as follows, so the team as a whole understands and evolves the needs into full-fledged requirements:

- The start of the analysis phases
- The start of the design phase
- Toward the end of the design phase and a few weeks before User Acceptance Testing (UAT)

The start of the analysis phase is when you are planned, prepared, and ready to start elicitation activities. You have identified the right stakeholders (limit the number of participants from 10 to 12, excluding the IT team). As much as possible, have an in-person session in a good size conference room. Participants being present in one location helps you understand clues from their non-verbal communication and helps everyone focus on the task at hand.

Plan the sessions and provide the agenda to all participants in advance. Set expectations for the session and as a group what you are all trying to get out of it. Make sure you keep slots for breakout sessions. Remember, not all sessions need all stakeholders.

During the start of the analysis phase, schedule the first session. The agenda and rules of engagement have to be very clear. As a business analyst, your job is to facilitate the conversation, manage conflict when things get out of control, and ask the right questions. You have to rephrase and ask questions till you and the participants understand the response and the need. There will be conflicting viewpoints on some requirements, which is natural. You can pause there and go on to the next requirement. During the breakout session, you can have a conversation with individuals with conflicting views and hash it out. Sometimes you have to escalate it to project and functional managers if a consensus is not reached. You are here to understand business needs, not to please everyone.

The team can use whiteboards/flip charts to put their ideas in visual form. It is an iterative process so let it keep going. Remember not to let conversations get sidetracked. Time is of the essence here and you need to manage it well. Once a requirement is understood, rather than putting that directly onto your tablet/book, I advise you (or one of the scribes) to write it on a flip chart, so that everyone can see it. Keep adding agreed requirements one after the other on the flip chart and let it be legible and visible to all during the duration of the session.

On the last day, make sure you sum up and read through the requirements loud and clear, and see if anyone has questions or concerns. Their body language will offer great clues and you can speak to them offline and clarify any concerns they have. Summarize the session and thank them for their participation and invaluable input. Provide a high-level agenda and schedule for the next session. Within the next business day, make sure you create a document with all the agreed requirements for all the participants and their managers. As needed, any open queries around any of the requirements are to be addressed in the next one to two weeks.

Prototyping

This technique will be most suitable for developing completely new processes/systems with brand new features and functions. The users may not be able to conceptualize exactly how they want the end product to be. Prototyping helps with a mock-up – an early sample of a build to test the concept, it helps identify early what it should not be.

Prototyping can be as simple as whiteboarding. The complete process is a screen flow on a whiteboard/flip chart with integration and automation captured in swim lane diagrams with various actors. This is an excellent collaboration technique where every team member should be given enough opportunities to comment and edit.

As an example, in one of my past projects, partner relationship management (**PRM**) was a brand-new functionality in Salesforce. We were one of the first companies to implement PRM. Our channel partner business would like a tool for customers to be able to search for partner contacts from the company website. The requirement was very vague at that time as we could not get much help from the vendor or consulting company we employed.

There are two types of prototypes:

- **Low fidelity**: These are quick and easy ways to visualize the outline of the proposed solution. Examples are wireframes, screen mock-ups, whiteboards, and flip charts.

- **High fidelity**: A mostly finished product with most of the features and functions. This can be utilized for pilot programs and later can be incorporated into the actual solution. In software, this evolves into the final design solution.

Process models

Process models help business analysts understand the current business processes and help model the future desired "to-be" processes. This model helps the stakeholder understand their current business process model. You can do it on a whiteboard or flipchart either by drawing with markers or using post-it notes. This will help stakeholders pitch in and point out or rearrange post-it notes if any activity is misarranged. Unless we understand the current "as-is" process flow, we will never be able to understand or identify the gaps. Once you and the stakeholders get to understand the current process clearly, you can start building the desired process flow models with the stakeholder, so that both parties agree on the desired model.

After you create the quick and dirty models, you can refine them and transfer them as permanent artifacts using the tool of your choice. I prefer to use the Visio tool to create the process flow and then socialize the Visio process flows in PDF format to stakeholders and get their feedback and agreement. These artifacts will be extremely useful for future projects and for creating and developing test scripts for testing.

User stories

User stories are a popular technique to write user requirements from the actual user role perspective. There are three main elements to a user story – who, what, and why? User stories are most often used during Agile project methodology:

As a *<Who = user role>*

I want *<What = to do something>*

So that I can *<Why = achieve a specific need or goal>*

The user role represents a type of user (for example, sales specialist, employee, investment banker, etc.). What is the action that the user wants to perform (for example, submitting a timesheet)? The last part of the user stories is the purpose of the action (for example, I can get paid).

The benefit of a user story is that the business, as well as the technical team, shall be able to understand and be able to get a good idea of requirements.

We shall make sure user stories are written clearly and have no ambiguity. Every user story should have clearly defined and mutually agreed-on acceptance criteria and the definition of done. Verify and validate that each of your user stories is independent of other user stories, is negotiable, adds value to your stakeholder upon implementation, can be estimated by your technical team, is small enough to contain in itself, and contains enough information that it can be tested.

Let me share with you a few examples.

The first example is partner registrations in the Salesforce system. Partner users should be able to register and gain access to their account and be able to access the Salesforce Partner portal. The business need, in this case, is to automate the complete process of Partner user creation. I drew this with workshop participants' input on a whiteboard. We refined it until we all agreed on what the business wanted. Later, we documented this in MS Word and added it as a document requirement addendum. This simple flow helped stakeholders. Project team members understood this complex business process in very simple visual terms.

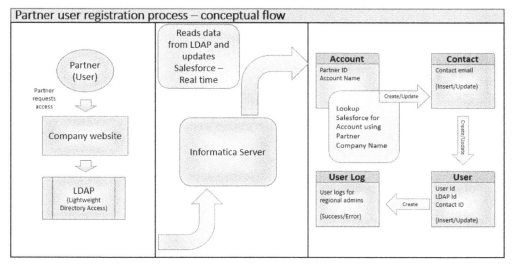

Figure 2.1 – Partner user registration process – conceptual flow

This second example is the account registration process. This is done during a conference room pilot session where we have stakeholders and technical team members. We captured all our thoughts collaboratively and came up with the swim lane diagram on a large whiteboard. Our team loved this process flow so much that they requested that I take a copy of the drawing "as is." The following flow was hand-drawn and you can do the same too. I found this process very collaborative and it excites participants as they are part of developing the process.

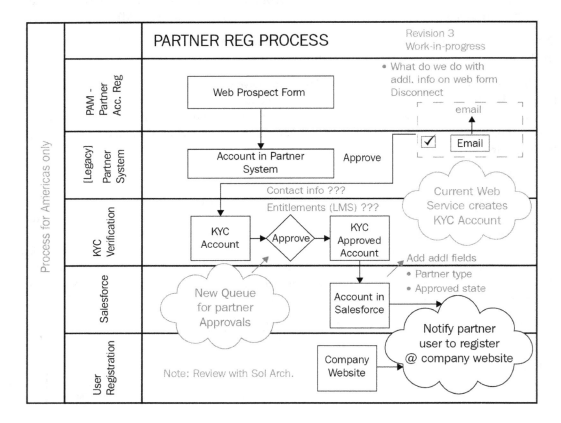

Figure 2.2 – Account registration process swim lane diagram

Example 3 (shown in *Figure 2.3*) shows a process flow where users will be able to create multiple product opportunities under one global opportunity. The production opportunities can be created by multiple product teams.

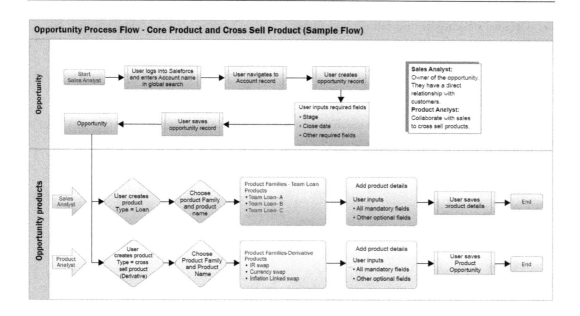

Figure 2.3 – Salesforce opportunity process flow

So far, we have discussed a few elicitation techniques that I found very helpful for my elicitation activities. There are numerous techniques available, and you can use ones that suit you. To draw out the needs of users, you have to use more than one technique. As needed, you conduct more elicitation activities to gain a complete detailed understanding of the requirements. So far, you have captured a wealth of information from various sources, now it is time for you to distill all the information and capture the essence of the needs and wants into documented requirements. Let us explore what you can do from your end to create this artifact.

Requirement documentation

So far, you have captured notes on the users' needs and wants. These are all the potential requirements – they are still vague and need structure so that they can be understood by both the stakeholder as well as your technical, testing, and training team. Our job is to transform and document them into high-quality, well-formatted requirements. The final documented requirements we produce will be well-written, clear, concise, and descriptive enough to avoid conflicts and confusion.

For stakeholder and project team members to be able to understand the requirement consistently in the same way, the requirement shall be written in to conform to the following attributes:

- Unambiguous
- Testable

- Original stakeholder understands and agrees
- Conforms to fit criteria
- Provides rationale
- Reviewed and agreed for completeness by technical and test leads

For documenting requirements, there are many templates available and your organization may have standard templates. The key attributes that you need to make sure you capture are the following:

- Requirement ID
- Objective
- User role
- Description
- Rationale
- Alternative scenario
- Assumptions
- Acceptance criteria
- Fit criteria
- Requestor name
- Document date
- Business Unit

The art of elicitation

Elicitation activity is a combination of art and science. Science in the sense that you need tools and techniques to keep you to be organized and help you identify, capture, and understand what the users want and need. Art in the sense of subtly getting the true essence of the business requirements that provide meaningful information that adds anticipated short- and long-term benefits.

Getting the facts requires planning, practice, discipline, skill, and of course a lot of hard work. Let me list a few of the skills that I felt you may find useful:

- Understand your stakeholders. Get to know their strengths, influences, likes, dislikes, hobbies, and so on. You need to connect with the users to be able to gain their trust.
- Plan well in advance. Go with a purpose. You need to understand the culture, business, technology, and how they operate.

- Prepare and plan your conversation tailored to the participant's style. Have the right set of questions and prepare scenarios on how to ask the questions intelligently.

- Listen actively to both verbal and non-verbal clues. You need to be comfortable with periods of silence when interacting with participants so that they can formulate their business needs, and allow them to fill in the blanks.

- Ask the right questions and show interest in learning from the users. If you show interest in their area of expertise, they will not be able to stop their urge to share their knowledge.

- Structure your conversation and try to see the big picture before getting into details. Try to facilitate an intelligent conversation.

- Make sure your elicitation sessions flow smoothly without any interruptions or distractions. It is all about the flow of what is in the minds of users. This means keeping note-taking activity to a minimum but taking enough notes to jog your memory later.

- Some end users try hard to convince you of their requirements to get into the limelight. They exaggerate and embellish. You need to be observant of these users and make sure these requirements are verified and agreed upon by other users.

To become good at elicitation, you need practice. Keep practicing and it becomes second nature. These are the soft skills that make you better at understanding your true needs. During some elicitation sessions, you may not get any meaningful information and this is perfectly fine. Keep calm and stay focused. You usually get the most insight just before concluding a good conversation. The three most important questions you should ask just before concluding the elicitation session are the following:

- What else can you tell me?

- What else did I miss?

- What else do you know?

You will be surprised how much valuable information and insight you will be able to obtain.

Practical tips for success

Here are some tips that will help you with elicitation activities. I make a checklist of these tasks so that I remember to implement them as much as possible.

- Be an active listener – be able to understand the meaning behind the work and the user's intentions.

- Understand the user needs in the context and be technology agnostic.

- Avoid stakeholders telling you what to do (solution) rather than what they need.

- Adopt incremental approaches where possible to foster innovative solutions and better solutions.

- Take notes… lots of them. Tag the source where you got the information. At a later date, if you need clarification, it helps you identify the source easily.

- Use visuals as much as possible to bring everyone to a common understanding.

- Communicate – send the minutes to all stakeholders, including the visuals and solicit feedback.

- Thank your stakeholders and team members for their participation. A good way to thank people is to take them out for a team outing or dinner. This helps with team building too.

- Provide feedback to participants' managers if someone went above and beyond. Recognition is a very strong tool and it motivates and encourages participation.

Summary

In this chapter, we covered elicitation planning. You learned about different tools and techniques of elicitation and that you have to use more than one tool and technique to bring forth requirements. Now you know that you need to take as many notes as possible so as not to lose any valuable information, and then take all this knowledge and write great requirements. You transform business users' expressed and unexpressed intentions, thoughts, and ideas, and document clear, crisp formalized requirements that eventually add value to all your stakeholders.

In the next chapter, we will take these requirements and work on prioritizing them. We will cover techniques that you can use that help you prioritize your requirements so that the technical team can add value during solution design and development activities.

Questions

1. How often do you do requirement elicitation?

2. What are some of the most important tasks during elicitation?

3. Can you recollect different tasks to perform during the elicitation phase to make it productive?

Further reading

- The PMI Guide to Business Analysis, PMI (`https://www.pmi.org/pmbok-guide-standards/foundational/business-analysis`)

3
Prioritizing Requirements

In the previous chapter, we learned about elicitation planning and the different tools and techniques of elicitation. You got the opportunity to transform the business user's expressed and unexpressed intentions, thoughts, and ideas into formalized requirements. You have a complete list of clear, consistent, complete, and validated requirements. Now, we need to review and sift through this huge list of requirements and work on prioritizing them. We have limited resources and we cannot deliver everything. To enable businesses to realize optimum business value by addressing the most pressing and important requirements, we need some kinds of prioritized requirements. For this, we need to identify the requirements that are valuable and group them.

In this chapter, you will learn about the process of managing requirement prioritization based on urgency and relative importance. You will work with the stakeholder/subject matter experts and rank requirements that are identified during the requirement identification phase. You will learn about the methods to identify important tasks that provide business value. You will also learn about the dependency map between various requirements and how to prioritize dependencies without creating gaps in the requirements flow. We will conclude this chapter by reviewing proven techniques for managing meetings, resolving conflicts, and getting consensus and agreement from stakeholders.

We will be covering the following topics:

- The importance of requirement prioritization
- Reviewing various prioritization techniques
- Creating a dependency map between requirements
- Managing prioritization meetings and getting consensus
- Simple CRM requirement prioritization and roadmap scenario

Requirement prioritization enables you to identify the most important business needs so that the next phase of the project can work on these important requirements. The most challenging task is how, as a business analyst, you manage conflicting priorities based on stakeholders having different goals and priorities. It is highly recommended to initiate ranking or staking requirements from the elicitation phase itself. From my experience, by starting early, you may easily identify about 50% of the top priorities that you think may go into the first release. Prioritization helps you plan the implementation and layout of the roadmap.

The importance of requirement prioritization

Any project has a limited budget, definite duration, and finite resources. Prioritization helps with managing requirements and the allocation and utilization of resources effectively and productively. It helps us focus on putting our efforts into implementing the most critical requirements that matter most. By prioritizing, we are identifying and defining when requirements get addressed and implemented. This helps us improve communications and keep everyone transparent. Many times, I have experienced that the prioritized list keeps changing. When socialized with stakeholders, they rethink and redefine what they need now versus later. This helps us to move requirements around and prioritize them to get the most benefit for everyone.

Prioritization activity should be iterative, at our workplace, we revisit this list every 3 to 6 months and adjust it based on the needs at that point in time. New requirements will be added and they may take higher priority, whereas the existing prioritized ones may be dropped as we found a new way to better address the needs. This list also helps us in creating project/product roadmaps. You can group them into various releases, such as numbers 1 to 10 from the prioritized list go into Release-1, numbers 11 to 20 go into Release-2, and so on. Sales and service team members do not have the patience to wait for years to see the solution, especially with Salesforce implementations. After we get the agreed prioritized list, we create a roadmap for the next 12 to 15 months, spacing releases every 3 to 6 months depending on the complexity of the deliverables. Good prioritization helps us with building these roadmaps and this, in turn, helps us plan project activities and keep stakeholders informed on when they can see the finished working product.

Reviewing prioritization techniques

To enable effective requirement prioritization processes to happen, we need to use objective consensus methods to remove any bias. Let us look at some of the frameworks that we can utilize. Sometimes, you have to use a combination of frameworks to achieve results.

These frameworks will aid you and your stakeholders in better decision-making. None of the techniques can work in isolation and it needs to be a collaborative effort. Understanding the available techniques will help you pick one that provides the most actionable results.

The following are some of the techniques/frameworks. Use the ones that work best for you:

- **The MoSCoW method**: Used to identify and action important requirements.
- **Multivoting**: Voting requirements based on an established set of rules/voting ranks that are point-based/cumulative.

- **Weighted ranking/staked ranking**: Ranking requirements based on established risk factors and weightage.

- **SWOT analysis**: Prioritizes based on **strengths, weaknesses, opportunities, and threats**.

- **RICE scoring**: Prioritizes based on scoring each requirement against these four factors: **reach, impact, confidence, and effort**.

- **Value versus effort**: Compares scores based on value, benefit, impact to cost, risk, complexity, and effort.

- **Story mapping**: Orders requirements on a grid in a logical manner to describe the activities end to end. This offers simplicity and is easy to understand.

You need to employ more than one method to get to the correct prioritizations.

I often use the MoSCoW method, weighted ranking, and story mapping for prioritizing my requirements. This is what I prefer to do:

1. Use a combination of methods to bucket them into three groups: High, Medium, and Low (or you can call them Red, Blue, and Yellow). This task can be achieved fairly quickly in a day or two provided it is done properly with the right set of team members in the session.

2. Get consensus and agreement from everyone that the requirements prioritized are categorized in the right bucket.

3. Next, we go through each one of the High-priority bucket items and use one or more of these prioritization techniques to rank them from 1 to N (with 1 being the highest priority).

4. Review them again after they are ranked collectively and agree on the ranking priorities. Do the same for Medium and Low. See the following diagram for more information:

Prioritized Buckets							
Priority 1			**Priority 2**			**Priority 3**	
Bucket 1 (3 Month Release)			Bucket 2 (6 Month Release)			Bucket 3 (3 Month Release)	
Priority	**Requirement**		**Priority**	**Requirement**		**Priority**	**Requirement**
1	Function -A		1	Function -D		1	Function -H
2	Function -B		2	Function -E		2	Function -I
3	Function -C		3	Function -F		3	Function -J
			4	Function -G			

Figure 3.1 – Prioritized requirements with each priority subprioritized

Next, we lay it on our roadmap. Based on time, budget, and resource availability, we pick X number of prioritized requirements for each release. In practice, some of the High-priority requirements will fall in Release-2. This is when the team needs to work collaboratively and see which ones are needed during Release-1 and which ones can wait until Release-3. Most conflicts arise in this kind of situation, as reality does not meet the perceived expectation. You, as a savvy business analyst, with the help of the project sponsor and project manager, need to show your negotiation skills and get everyone on the same page to agree. It's not that these techniques or methods produce a well-prioritized list, it is the team that does that collaboratively. You can use one or more of these techniques or your own techniques.

The following figure shows an example of a multi-year roadmap for a sample of prioritized requirements. Adding a roadmap element to your requirement prioritization activity sets expectations with stakeholders and project team members and keeps the overall requirement process transparent:

Project Roadmap -FY22/FY23								
	FY2022				FY2023			
Roadmap	Q1	Q2	Q3	Q4	Q1	Q2	Q3	Q4
Release -1	Priority 1 Function A,B,C							
Release -2		Priority 2 Function D,E,F,G						
Release -3				Priority 3 Function H,I,J				
Release -4					Priority 4 Function K,L,M,N,O			
Release -5							Priority 5 Function P,Q,R	

Figure 3.2 – FY2022/FY2023 Multi-year project roadmap

Let us review some of these techniques. We are not getting into details as that is not the aim of this chapter.

MoSCoW analysis

The **MoSCoW analysis** categorization (or **MSCW** excluding vowels) stands for **must have, should have, could have,** and **would have**:

- **Must haves:** These requirements are needed, and without these, the project does not exist. Enabling these needs helps the business unit achieve its goals. These are the core functionality and capabilities of the system. For example, an account management functionality where users can create and edit customer records in a system. Also, if this is security risk-related or compliance mandated, then it will fall under this category.

- **Should haves**: These requirements are important and valuable and can wait a little longer. You will need them soon but not immediately. Examples are workflow notifications, automating processes, and so on. Users can still utilize the system but may need to rely on manual processes, which is inconvenient but possible. These requirements are also important and need to follow after all the must-haves are completed.

- **Could have**: These requirements pose a minimal impact on the project at this time. For example, a user would like to see their attributes (such as owner's region/country/division/department) in account and contact records. Most of the time, these are simple requests and can be clubbed with one of the previous two categories to get synergy by saving time during the design, testing, and deployment. Of course, you still need to develop and do some level of design work.

- **Would have**: These requirements have no impact for now and do not impact the project. These are more ideas that may eventually morph into more important requirements and move up the chain. Examples are cosmetic changes to the UI or email templates.

Story mapping

In this technique, we arrange user stories for an end-to-end process in a sequence in a specific order of importance. By reviewing the stories along the process from start to finish, both the critical paths and possible alternate paths, we will be able to identify gaps as well as stories in the wrong position or undesired stories along the way. This will help during the prioritizing session in rearranging the stories for a more effective future state. This is like connecting all the dots to make a complete picture. When you see the end-to-end big picture, you can easily see the missing, misplaced, and redundant dots.

This method also lets us map the dependencies, such as the connection between the stories in the sequence of flow. Story mapping helps us find missing or unwanted events, which in turn helps us to refine prioritization. If managed well, story mapping gets the best outcome by complementing each other with other techniques.

A sample story mapping event flow is shown in *Figure 3.3*:

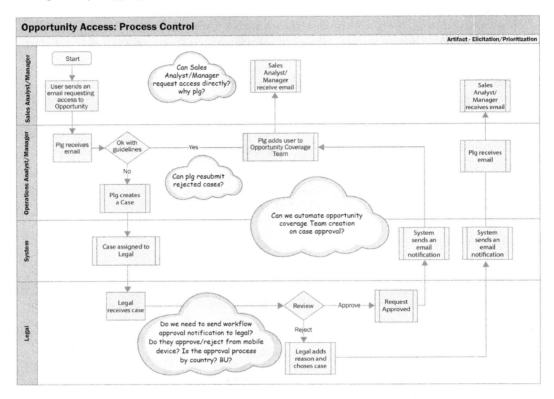

Figure 3.3 – Story mapping business event flow with missing requirements

For simplification purposes, we added only the story name and depicted this in the process flow format. When discussing with stakeholders, you can write each event on a story card and rearrange the story cards until you have the most optimal story that fits your business needs. You can think of each activity as a story card. This rearrangement will automatically give you the right priority for each of the story cards.

Now you know there are different prioritizing techniques, and you can pick ones that suit your project. In the next section, let us review and see how we can establish dependencies between requirements.

Dependency map between requirements

There exist functional dependencies between requirements, either from the same projects or from other project initiatives, and this will lead to reprioritizing requirements. We need to identify cross-functionality dependencies and prioritize requirements to align them by understanding dependencies between processes, systems, and teams.

You can identify requirements dependencies by reviewing or creating end-to-end process flows, function and system diagrams, and conceptual flows.

In this example, let us assume we have requirements from **A** to **J**, as listed in *Figure 3.4*, with priority values from **1** to **10**. We stack-ranked them in our first iteration and in the second iteration, we used the dependency mapping technique and discovered that two specific requirements are linked together and need to be implemented at the same time; if not, neither will work:

Option 1		Option 2		Option 3	
Priority	**Requirement**	**Priority**	**Requirement**	**Priority**	**Requirement**
1	A	1	A	1	Ax
2	B	2	F	2	B
3	C	3	B	3	C
4	D	4	C	4	D
5	E	5	D	5	E
6	F	6	E	6	Ay+F
7	G	7	G	7	G
8	H	8	H	8	H
9	I	9	I	9	I
10	J	10	J	10	J

Figure 3.4 – Requirement prioritization options

Let us analyze this step by step.

Option 1 is our first draft of prioritized requirements. We discovered that requirements **A** and **F** are interdependent. Implementing this option makes **A** unusable unless **F** is implemented.

We have multiple ways to address this dependency. For simplicity reasons, let's say we came up with two other options.

Move **F** next to **A** and implement priorities **1** and **2** together as one unit. Now you are knocking others down. This is **Option 2**.

If feasible, split **A** into **Ax** (independent part) and **Ay** (dependent part with **F**), so that **Ax** can be done now, and **Ay** and **F** later. This is **Option 3**.

As an example, look at the following two separate requirements:

- Account management functionality: Sales analysts shall be able to create, update, and transact with the customers (High priority).
- Integrate customer identity verification so that sales analysts can verify customer identity. Sales analysts shall be able to access identifying information from the different systems without the need for a separate login (Medium priority).

On further analysis, we discovered that sales analysts cannot transact with customers without verifying customer identification. There is a dependency between these two requirements.

A possible solution is that we can make it into two parts:

- Enable user-friendly customer identification hyperlinks on the customer page. When the user clicks on the link, it opens up a window requesting them to add their credentials to access the system.

- Enable **single sign-on** (**SSO**) functionality shortly after release and make the hyperlink SSO-enabled.

We can identify this kind of dependency issue by using prioritization techniques such as dependency maps and be able to find workarounds. After addressing the dependency, we can reprioritize and adjust requirement priorities to get the most benefit.

Managing prioritization meetings

We reviewed various prioritization techniques and now you are equipped with different prioritization tools. In this section, let us look at how to make the process better by effectively managing the prioritization meetings.

For the requirement prioritization meetings, only key members need to be present in this meeting. Examples include the lead business analyst, technical lead, architect, project manager, cross-functional leads, key SMEs, project sponsors, and stakeholders. The technical team, architects, and project managers will be observers and will need to contribute when their expertise is needed for confirmation and clarification. Usually, the team size should be approximately 10 to 12 people and it's highly recommended that they are co-located in a conference room. This is not an elicitation session and you do not need to have all team members present.

These are key decision-making events where leads/managers decide what is needed, when it is needed, and how it is needed for the business unit. The management can greatly benefit as this prioritized list will be the input for an implementation roadmap for the next 1, 2, or 3 years.

You can make prioritization meetings meaningful and effective, as follows:

- Engagement rules should be communicated
- Prioritization meetings should be well planned and communicated
- Clear agenda and goals should be communicated
- Ground rules for conflict resolutions should be established
- Educate and give an overview of the tools and techniques the team plan to use

- Define the criteria for prioritizing factors and their weights
- Set up a good conference room with a large wall-to-wall whiteboard, flipcharts, and projector to display previously created process flows, conceptual flows, and so on

Factors you need to take into account while prioritizing are as follows:

- **Statutory/regulatory**: As an example, if it is mandated by the regulatory authority, these have to be prioritized very highly. For example, data encryption at REST for PII data on account and contact records in Salesforce.

- **Policy-related/audit findings**: These are required by the company. It may be a policy to restrict emails from going to external users when sending notifications from the Salesforce system. Or it can be related to an audit finding that needs to be remediated at the earliest.

- **Cost to implement**: This can be any reason such as consulting costs for specific skills being too high. Specific vendor software can be easy to implement and use.

- **Time to implement**: Can this be implemented quickly in 3- to 4-month windows or does it need a long time?

- **Value to users**: Does it add value? Can it save users time, help them do things better and faster, or give them a better user experience?

- **Benefit to organization/business unit**: Does it meet regulatory requirements or get a better ROI?

- **Ease of technology use**: Can the system be used by end users relatively easily with minimal training or can it be scaled for more users?

- **Skills availability**: Do we have skilled team members? If we have to customize a specific function, do we have that skill set? For example, to create a complex function, do we have a skill set in Salesforce Apex and knowledge of Tableau CRM?

- **Conflicting requirements**: Implementing one will prohibit the other from implementing.

Based on your project, you can use combinations of these factors. Also, the relative importance of each factor may vary between projects and between companies. During the elicitation phase, plan and obtain agreements on the prioritization procedure to make decisions on what takes priority. Make every effort to see whether you can move forward constructively and negotiate a compromise with stakeholders with conflicting priorities or requirements. Establish a conflict escalation and resolution mechanism. Justify why a specific requirement is prioritized as High and another one is rejected. Be open, truthful, and transparent, and communicate the decision as early as possible to all stakeholders.

Based on the project, culture, stakeholders, and other parameters, rather than ranking, prioritize them in groups. All requirements that belong to a group will have the same rank and they will be implemented and released together.

Practical tips for success

Let us take a look at a few pointers that might help you with your prioritization activities. They are very useful and important and can potentially save you a lot of pain and time:

- Manage expectations by progressive prioritization and by being transparent.

- Set expectations with stakeholders that not all requirements may be implemented.

- Ask the right question:

  - What problem are we trying to solve?

  - What happens if we implement it?

  - What happens if we do not implement it?

- Involve the right stakeholder who is relevant to a specific session. For example, if you are discussing the account management process, there is no value in inviting all quote/contract management stakeholders.

- Not all stakeholders are the same. Some have a bigger say on what to prioritize because of their rank, knowledge, role, and so on.

- Whenever you reprioritize, make sure you are not breaking something else. You need to re-run whatever technique you used before, plus at least one more technique.

- Some requirements have to be prioritized as High because they may differentiate your product compared to other competitor products for political reasons (such as you want to release the feature for a major conference), and improve adoption/usability (if adoption and usability are already an issue).

- Prioritizing high-risk requirements early will help you mitigate the risk and find alternative options in the event it does not work out.

- You have to implement some requirements that may have a lower priority. We create a **minimum viable product** (**MVP**) and implement only the core functionality with minimal effort, which can be enhanced later. This effort will help you gain their trust and create excitement and interest. Do it wisely. Your main opposition will be your project manager.

- Start prioritizing efforts early. Start tagging them as High, Medium, or Low. Keep reviewing them iteratively and keep the document current. Priorities change as the requirements age.

Simple CRM requirement prioritization and roadmap scenario

Here is a real-life scenario that will help you get an idea of how to keep the stakeholder informed and set expectations. I simplified the functions so that it will be easier for you to understand and get a gist of it. The following screenshot is our documented requirements at the end of the elicitation activity. In these scenarios on the left, we have functionality for **Account Management**, **Contact Management**, and **Opportunity Management** in groups:

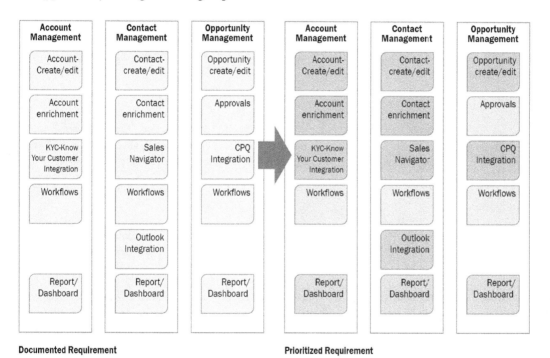

Figure 3.5 – Prioritizing requirements [before --> after]

Now, we took the documented requirements and color-coded priorities during prioritizing sessions with key stakeholders. We used ranking and story mapping techniques and came up with bucket ranking (Red – Priority 1, Aqua – Priority 2, Gold – Priority 3, and Green – Priority 4) on the right-hand side.

Let's review the rationale:

- Priority 1:

  - Core functionality such as Account, Contact, and Opportunity Management are our main goals. Without these, we cannot implement anything else.

  - Compliance and regularity requirements such as **Know Your Customer** (**KYC**) identifies customer confirmation, and this is a complex process that resides in the external system.

- Priority 2:

  - Workflows (automation, notifications, and approval) are our next business priority to get informed and take timely action. This will enable us to have a better user experience and better adoption.

- Priority 3:

  - Data enrichment tool (for example, D&B Hoovers, Pitchbook, and Demand Tools), sales navigator (for example, LinkedIn sales tool for contact enrichment), and integration. These tools and integrations automate and simplify data creation. Our priority here is to keep the data clean, usable, and relevant.

- Priority 4:

  - After we have the core functions, good data, integrations, and automation, we implemented reports and a dashboard. Our rationale here is to enable a tool that works accurately. So, it made sense for us to have it after data enrichment.

Now we have the prioritized list, nicely colored and agreed upon by all stakeholders, which mapped each of the requirements to their appropriate priority. All is well with everyone so far, as some stakeholders with Priority 2 requirements may expect to get theirs implemented along with Priority 1 during the first release. Even worse, some stakeholders may expect even Priority 3s and 4s to be delivered during the first release. So how do we solve this?

Your next task is to place them in release buckets. Before segregating them into buckets, educate stakeholders about the release timeline, resource capacity, high-level time estimate, effort, and so on. Once everyone agrees, start dropping each requirement into various buckets starting with the highest priority to the lowest. In our simplified example, we moved all Priority 1s into release bucket 1. If you still have the capacity, you can move some of the Priority 2s into this bucket. Finally, you will be able to assign all requirements into various releases after long conversations, agreements, and disagreements. The following figure depicts the roadmaps for your requirements. This gives a glance at when a user can expect to see their requirement implemented:

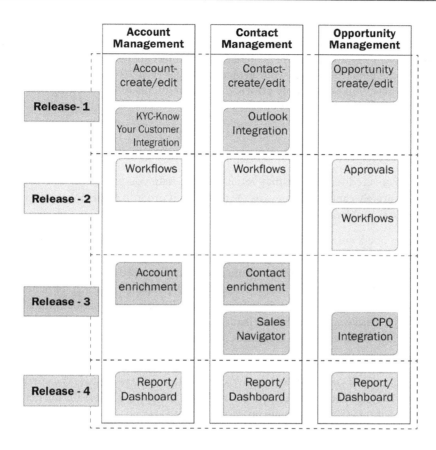

Figure 3.6 – Requirements roadmap

This analysis is specific to the project. Your priorities may be different from the ones we have, even though we both have similar Salesforce implementations. As a business analyst, you have the knowledge and experience of navigating your organization and getting requirement priorities that fit your requirements.

Business analysis and project management in a true sense go by strict rules and are very stringent on what is in scope and what is not. On paper, this is all well and good, but in real work, this is not the way it works. I have seen many requests prioritized as low and these are requested by influential stakeholders and end users. 80% of these requests take only 20% of the time. Rather than wasting time on negotiations, I would go with re-prioritizing and tagging this 80% with other higher priority items. By logically grouping them, you save time during testing, training, and deployment. At the end of the day, we deliver more with a little bit more effort, but at the same time, gain the trust of stakeholders. This helped me tremendously in my later projects as these stakeholders understand that you do what is best, and since they trust you, the business analysis process gets more impactful and fun.

> **Note**
> While some may argue that project managers are responsible for project roadmaps with input from all key players, I would say there is no harm in business analysts initiating and creating one. Later, you can hand this over to your **project manager** (PM). By creating this during the prioritization phase, you are not only prioritizing requirements but also letting users know when they will get their requirements addressed.

Summary

In this chapter, we covered techniques that you can use to help you prioritize your requirements so that you can accurately capture business needs in the right order of priority, keeping the process transparent for all stakeholders.

You got a good idea of why requirement prioritization is important and how it helps you to identify the most important requirements that the team should address to fulfill the business need and add value. We looked at various prioritization techniques that can be used to enable the team with the prioritization process. We also showed you how to create a dependency roadmap of requirements to help you identify any gaps and opportunities to improve by adding new requirements or re-arranging existing requirements. Finally, we learned about managing prioritization meetings and getting consensus, helping you to manage conflicts, obtain consensus from all participants, and keep stakeholders up to date with the requirement priorities.

In the next chapter, we will cover process flow. We will review how to capture the current state of business and what the gaps and opportunities are, and then develop a process for the desired future state. We will also capture ways to automate processes so that users can have a great user experience.

Questions

1. What are conflicting requirements and can we implement these requirements?
2. What are the advantages and disadvantages of the MoSCoW technique?
3. Why is requirement prioritization important?

Further reading

- *Requirements Management: A Practice Guide by PMI*: (`https://www.pmi.org/pmbok-guide-standards/practice-guides/requirements-management`)

4

Process Flows – "As-Is" versus "To-Be"

In the previous chapter, we learned about the importance of prioritization, various prioritization techniques, mapping requirements dependencies, and finally managing requirements prioritization meetings. We can successfully create a list of prioritized requirements that accurately reflect our business needs in the optimal order of priorities so that the most valuable needs are addressed first.

This chapter explains the importance of business process flow – procedures and information flows – and analyzes the gaps and opportunities. The "as-is" flow helps you capture current existing business process flows and any underlying gaps. From here, you will learn how to develop the "to-be" business process flow by plugging the gaps in the "as-is" flow. We also will discuss how you can identify opportunities and automate information flow via backend automation and workflows.

In this chapter, we will cover the following topics:

- Reviewing the process flow
- Understanding and capturing the current state "as-is"
- Proven techniques to capture the current state
- Identifying gaps and improvement/automation opportunities
- Developing the future state – "to-be"

By the end of this chapter, you will have learned effective ways to capture process flows, starting with the current state "as-is," and then morphing this into the future state "to-be" process flow while understanding various steps and their dependencies and sequence. You will be equipped with the knowledge, tools, and techniques through real-life practical examples so that you can adopt these practices while creating your process flows.

Reviewing the process flow

A process flow is a workflow diagram of all the tasks/steps and their interconnection in a visual format. Depicting various steps in a process visually will help all stakeholders get a common understanding of the needs and, hence, the requirements.

Defining process flows is iterative: you start from the elicitation phase with very high-level process flows and keep refining during the prioritization phase until they are socialized and agreed upon by the stakeholders, SMEs, and technical team members. This business process flow will capture enough details in business terminology so that it is a process flow that all stakeholders understand. During the design and development phase, these flows can be refined so that the technical team and testing team can understand them in greater depth. The first thing we must do when we develop a process flow is have the right set of stakeholders and SMEs with in-depth knowledge of their current process. We do not invite all stakeholders like in the elicitation phase. We can use any fancy tools to capture the process flow, but for now, let us stick with our good old whiteboard (or flip charts). This will help with excellent collaboration. Later, once it is finalized, you can take a picture of the finalized drawing and create the flow in the Visio tool or any other BPM tool of your choice. Documenting the final version of the process flow will serve as an excellent project artifact that will be helpful to current and future users.

Process flows help identify inconsistencies, repetitions, roundabouts, missing steps, bottlenecks, and so on that are involved in a process. A methodical analysis of the "as-is" process flow helps a business analyst with the opportunity to think analytically, creatively, and innovatively about what the business user needs so that they can develop an effective "to-be" future state.

> **Note**
> There may be times when part of the project (or the entire project) may be put on hold after the analysis phases due to other priorities or a specific process map may not be adding intended value to the project. This means that, as a business analyst, you did your job well and helped the management decide upfront and save resources that can be utilized on other tasks. Documenting and storing these artifacts will result in saving project time and resources when management decides to reinitiate the project scope at a future date. It also helps existing users understand their process steps as well as the entire process flow.

Let us start with the current process – the "as-is" flow. If you have an existing flow, you can use that as your starting flow and develop it. However, if you do not have one, you can start from scratch. Do not worry about where to start. Start from somewhere, anywhere, and then keep adding steps. After you add a few boxes and the interconnections, when the workshop participants see the process coming to life visually, this will fuel creativity among the participants and they will keep adding more details. Keep the momentum and excitement going. From here, your job is to ask the right questions and encourage the team to collaborate. Do not stop or question the flow of user thoughts and their kindled creativity. We are here to capture the essence of the business process, and who else would be better at this than the users who perform those tasks? Give all the credit to them; this will be a great motivator for them to bring out their tacit knowledge. In the first iteration, have them draw anything and everything they can think of. You have time to query and get clarifications in subsequent iterations. It will take a few iterations before it falls in line with what you want to see and makes sense.

> **Note**
> A process is a sequence of activities. Each activity can be one or more tasks or steps. For simplicity, capture each task/step as a box and lines with arrows to depict the interconnection between various steps.

Process flow types

Let us look at some of the important types of process flows that you can develop. Knowing them and understanding their purpose will guide you in picking the right process flow type. Remember, we are not creating these process flows for documentation purposes; they go way beyond and help us achieve better user adoption. Our goal is to come up with a good process that your workshop participants understand and relate to:

- **Macro process map**: This provides understanding for the executive team and provides a management view of the process. This is very high level and should not contain any technical jargon. Use business jargon such as your company-specific terms so that business users can relate it to their business.

- **Business process flows**: These are the "as-is" and "to-be" process flows and can be understood by the business stakeholder and the end users. Refrain from using technical jargon as much as possible and use business-specific jargon as much as possible.

- **Architectural process flow**: These process flows are complex and highly technical, and mostly cross-functional and integration-related. This helps the technical and enterprise architecture teams understand the flow from a technology perspective so that they can capture the nonfunctional and non-human interface needs and requirements.

> **Note**
> **Standard Operating Procedures (SOPs)** are not process flows. They are step-by-step instructions for the end users to perform operational tasks in a production system. You can use various process flows and other artifacts to develop SOPs, whose goal is to make the process clear, efficient, and effective.

Understanding and capturing the current state "as-is"

To understand business needs, you need to understand how they are operated. What is the current process, regardless of whether you have it documented or not?

Let us start with a clean slate, assuming we do not have any existing artifacts. Each user knows their tasks and the process related to the task very well, but they do not have the bigger picture – that is, how other users do their tasks or how all related tasks are interlinked.

So, where do we start? The process of documenting any process appears to be complex and confusing and you may not know where to start. The simplest way is to get the right set of people and start drawing the process on a whiteboard or a flip chart. At this juncture, do not worry about what tool to use and what technique you need – just start drawing it. You need multiple iterations before you can get a good process flow that is well understood and approved by all stakeholders.

In the first iteration, you may not even go much further, but at least you will be able to lay out a simplified one from start to finish. Let all team members contribute to the flow. Capture any questions/queries/clarification/assumptions as your team collectively develops the flow. Make sure you keep a guardrail so that discussion sticks to the intended agenda topic while resolving any conflicts that arise along the way.

Let us look at the following example flow. This is one of the functionalities we implemented as part of Partner Relationship Management on the Salesforce Sales Cloud platform. Before the implementation, this registration process was performed using multiple legacy systems, including Excel, and many manual processes. To help you understand this, I have simplified this process and changed it:

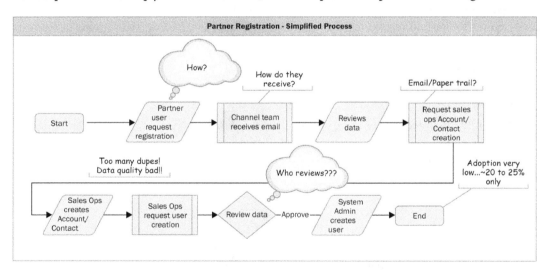

Figure 4.1 – Simplified process flow

This flow is for a partner user to request access and be able to get access to your system so that they can access the customers and related information:

1.   Your partner (channel partner) requests registration to your PRM system so that they can access customer data and do so collaboratively with your sales team.

2. The channel team receives a registration request from partners via manual email or over the phone.

3. A review process is involved before you can proceed with this information. During the first iteration, we do not know what this is, but we capture this so that we do not lose track. In subsequent iterations, we will refine this and add more meaning to this step.

4. The next step is requesting sales operations to create Account and Contact records (we do not have any details on who informs Sales Ops or how they are notified).

5. Sales Operations created the data. Since this is a manual entry and as we do not have any processes defined, this team often creates duplicates, which results in bad data quality.

6. Again, we have a review process and none of us know who does what as the process is not defined clearly. It takes too long for the process to complete and is a concern that was raised by almost all stakeholders as it is the major cause for delays in the overall process time.

7. Since user creation is an admin's job, Sales Ops request the admin to create a user and provide access to the account and related information such as contacts, opportunities, cases, quotes, and so on.

8. The process ends after creating a partner user record.

We can take these steps and start drawing boxes/arrows. During these phases, do not worry about what shape of box or line you use. Let your imagination flow freely and you can pretty much capture it in square boxes with some text and comments so that everyone participating understands them.

We also captured discussion items on this topic. During the first few cuts, let information and ideas flow. I have seen this process become more effective as more boxes and lines are added. Our users get excited when they see how their contribution impacts others, the process flow, and the business as a whole. This is like an "Aha!" moment for the users, where they see the complete picture for the very first time.

We will discuss how and why this technique helps us in many ways in the *Benefits of creating process flows* section.

You may be wondering when and how to start this activity. The answer is the sooner the better, and this is intertwined with all other activities. You take small steps and progressively build them with the help of various stakeholders and project team members. I usually start this activity during my elicitation phase, and progressively review and improve it during each phase. At this phase, we did not define who does what and the true dependencies. We merely captured all the business and functional tasks and sequenced them from start to finish. I usually do this during my workshop or conference room pilot sessions. At the end of the session, walk through the process from start to end, and along the way capture comments. Use different colored boxes, lines, and text to add clarity and to make the process flow more interesting.

Later, after the meeting is over, as soon as possible, take some time and capture exactly what was documented by the team on one of the BPM tools (or you can neatly draw them on white paper).

Reflect on the whole meeting and the notes you captured and check for overlooked tasks or steps. I prefer to use Microsoft Visio since I've been using it for a long time and find it easy to use and very useful. You can save this as a PDF file and send it to all the participants so that they can review it and come prepared for the next iteration. I mentioned PDFs here so that the users cannot modify and make multiple versions where it is difficult to track. Assign one person who will be responsible for creating the process flows so that you can communicate changes based on suggestions to all participants.

> **Note**
>
> I found it very useful to take a screen capture on my mobile device and send it to the participants. Since they are the ones who contributed and drew various steps, they feel proud and motivated to see their drawing. They tend to look at it more often and share it with their team.
>
> This process flow is conceptual. You get the concept of the process from end to end. Using this as a starting point during requirement activities will help you during elicitation, documentation, and prioritizing requirements. They are easy to draw and easy to visualize and follow through.

Current state swim lane process flow diagram

At this point, we are trying to capture how the end users use the system to perform their business tasks – that is, the existing end-to-end process flow. We are trying to find out what they do now in the present scenario, the essence of what they do, and why they do it that way. This can span boundaries, such as multiple systems and multiple cross-functional teams. We capture everything here, such as duplicates, redundancies, efficiencies, inefficiencies, automation, manual processes, gaps, opportunities, and so on. Remember, you do not have a say in the current process and it is what it is. Collaboratively, we are trying to understand how it operates.

Now, let us refine this further. We will use the simplified process flow diagram we developed earlier as the starting point for our more refined process flow. My choice of preference is a swim lane diagram flow chart to document who does what in the process flow. You can have vertical or horizontal swim lanes and you can pick whatever way works best for you and your team. If you do not prefer swim lanes, go with the simplified flow and keep refining it as you progress through the project phases:

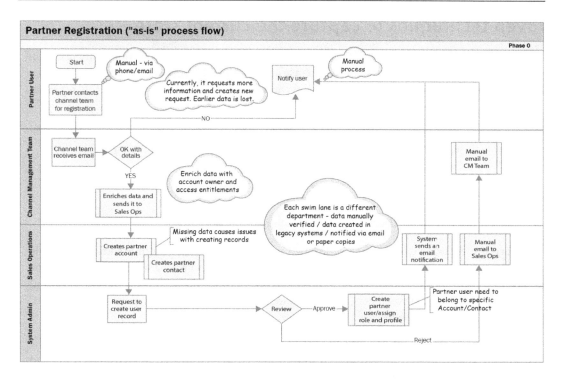

Figure 4.2 – Partner registration "as-is" process flow

In this diagram, we have a horizontal swim lane diagram. Each lane is tagged to a user role – the "who" part of it. For example, who does this task/step? The partner user requests registration and at various steps gets notifications/confirmations. We take our simplified flow and start stacking them in a sequence of tasks, as well as the user role, which is responsible for the activity. You cannot just jump from an earlier simplified process flow to this one in one swoop. It takes a few iterations and detailed reviews with stakeholders to come to this point. Our end goal is to capture every possible activity, how each respective role performs the activities, and the sequence of those activities from start to end. Socialize this flow with an extended team member and see if they have the same understanding as the team that prepared it. Accurately understanding and capturing these process flow steps helps stakeholders and project team members understand and elicit requirements in greater detail, and then turn them into a robust solution that meets the expectations of the business.

Do not look for 100% perfection and accuracy. Resources are limited, so you cannot keep on refining forever. We stop at a point where everyone agrees with some assumptions and constraints. With the given and available resources and timeline, we can come up with a process flow. It can certainly be improved but we stop here and don't move unless we see a major glitch in the flow. You will get the opportunity to refine this further in the next phase of the project.

Proven techniques to capture the current state

Understanding the current state helps us understand how things work now concerning existing opportunities and pain points and helps us enhance and optimize processes for improved outcomes. We utilize this current state process flow and optimize it to create a future flow. Let us see what techniques we can use to create process flows.

There are many techniques, some of which were discussed in *Chapter 2, Elicitation and Document Requirements*. I use the following techniques when developing process flow with my stakeholders:

- Observation
- Interviews/focus groups
- Conference room pilots/requirements workshops

My preferred method is workshops/conference room pilots, where you invite knowledgeable stakeholders who know their current ways of doing their business and have a wider knowledge of the industry. Engaging the right stakeholder, getting well prepared for the sessions with an agenda and goals, commitments from stakeholders, and open and honest collaboration will make the workshops/ conference room pilots very effective.

From these workshops, we can get very good start-to-finish process steps. You can supplement the process flow we've created so far by observing end users working through the steps in real life and see if those steps map to the developed process flows steps.

Also, for some complex to highly complex process steps, it will be beneficial for you to meet with experts in a focus group setting, where you can use your elicitation skills to understand the true need and essence of the process steps. The team may perceive certain steps to be redundant or duplicated, but the true essence is that those steps are required as a part of country-specific business requirements and regulatory or legal requirements. Not understanding these will affect the project adversely as you will have missed a critical pre-existing business need.

As a business analyst, I found this sequencing very helpful:

- Plan and schedule these sessions in such a way that you scheduled them logically. This depends on how much time you have and the availability of your stakeholders.
- I prefer to start and end with a workshop. This is where we invite all key stakeholders, and their validation and confirmation are key success factors.
- In between the workshops, plan the focus groups and observation sessions. You need specific experts who are responsible for performing specific steps and who only know that territory.
- The first session starts with the larger group of key stakeholders. Collectively, you all create the high-level process steps.

- Study the process steps that you created with the stakeholder group, analyze and research, and come up with the right set of questions about items where you need clarification or better understanding.

- Take up these questions with the smaller groups or by actually watching end users perform their jobs.

- Take plenty of notes and make sure you understand the process thoroughly.

- Facilitate a final session with key stakeholders (our original first session group) and walk them through the process. Update the group as needed based on findings from the focus group/observation.

- Finalize the current "as-is" process flow. After you finalize it, lock and publish this approved version to all project team members.

Your elicitation skills and collaboration with the right set of skilled stakeholders, coupled with these steps, will help add structure in capturing the current state process flow accurately.

Identifying gaps and improvement/automation opportunities

So far, we have created the current "as-is" process. We have a pretty good understanding of how things work. Now, let us see how we can identify bottlenecks and improvement opportunities in our existing process and refine the process flow.

Before we finalize the prioritization of this list of requirements, we have another iterative task of mapping them to the process flow steps that we created so far. Let us see how we can do this:

1. Map each requirement to one or more of the activities from the "as-is" process flow.

2. Sometimes, one requirement may map to more than one activity or set of tasks. For example, creating an account record generates an email to the owner of the record, as well as sends the data via web service call to your backend KYC system.

3. Not all requirements will map to the current process. This is expected as the new requirements mean new functionality that the business needs and we need to add new boxes to the flow diagram.

4. Some requirements require the addition of cross-functional connectors. For example, we want to send a quote on approval to the SAP system for contract generation. After the contract is generated in SAP, we must update the Salesforce quote with the contract ID before we can close it.

5. You may find duplicate steps on current process flows, which need deduping. Whether you add or remove a step, make sure you run through the whole process flow from start to finish so as not to break any functionality.

6. If you outrun all your requirements and still have some activities on process flow, you need to revisit requirements gathering. This means you missed some obvious requirements.

7. If you see dependent activities created by different teams on the process flow, this is the time to automate the specific activity. Automating helps keep the data clean and relevant. For example, when creating an opportunity from the Account record, say we would like to default the industry, sub-industry, owner country, owners' region, and account type so that users can view these fields on opportunity list view controls in salesforce. List view controls let users choose fields only if they are on that object. Rather than users keying the same data from an account on to opportunity, we can easily automate them.

8. After many activities on the process flow, we see notifications/emails that have been sent to user roles. This is a good opportunity for us to enhance the usability of this notification. For example, we can add a URL link to record the notification. By doing so, users can access records via email, where the URL will be provided, with a single click without the need to search for the record.

9. You can find a multitude of considerations that can add value. Can we use web calls to update data in real time rather than batch jobs?

As we can see, there are many benefits to visually representing the process. By combining this with other tools and techniques, stakeholders can understand and contribute more openly and honestly. In the next section, we will learn how to use this knowledge to identify gaps and opportunities and come up with a future state "to-be" process flow.

Developing the future state – "to-be"

Previously, we took the "as-is" process flow and identified some gaps and a few areas of improvement. We can add those sets to the process flow to create a "to-be" future state. When developing a "to-be" process flow, you and your stakeholder should be very clear on what future state you want to develop. Is this for phase 1, the project, or the entire project roadmap? If the roadmap is too long, you need to evaluate it and see if it makes sense to do so in digestible chunks. For example, you could create a future flow for phases 1 and 2. After these two phases have been implemented, based on users' feedback, you can start the next version of the process flow. This is especially true when you're implementing completely new business processes on a new software platform.

Remember to scope and think of usability and user experience. Better user experience translates into better usage and adoption, and this translates into greater value to the projects.

At each step in the process, think about some of the usability elements from the user's perspective:

- **Simplification**: How can we simplify this step in the process flow?

- **Automation**: Do we need the user to perform this step or can I automate this task?

- **Intuitiveness**: Is the screen flow designed in such a way that the user can intuitively perform the tasks with ease? Does the process guide the user?

- **Accessibility**: Does the user get a complete picture of what they do? For example, do they have a 360-degree view of the customer page?

Future state swim lane process flow diagram

Some of the enhancements/improvements we can add based on prioritized requirements are as follows:

- Able to add functionality for users to request registration from the company website rather than requesting via email.

- On submitting the web registration form, we can store the data in a custom object. This adds value if the partner has to submit more/corrected information or needs to resubmit the form with additional requested information.

- We can automate many workflow rules originating from the system.

- We can provide a confirmation ID to partners for future reference so that they can use this ID to obtain the status of their request.

- In case more data is required from the partner, we provided a link in the workflow notification so that the partner user can update the existing registration web form and resubmit the data.

- We can use table functions that potentially go into future phases/releases. These are placeholders and help stakeholders and project team members think about what is on the horizon.

- To improve adoption and usability, we highlighted the auto-creation of user records based on the domain address and enabled a **single sign-on** (**SSO**) feature.

Now, let us take a look at the future state "to-be" process flow after incorporating the necessary changes into the current state flow. A sample future flow with more streamlined and connected steps with automation is shown in the following diagram:

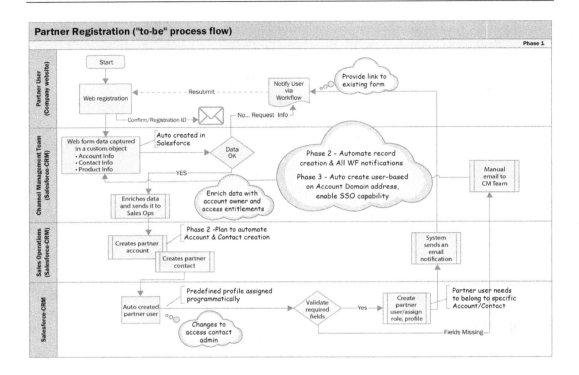

Figure 4.3 – Partner registration "to-be" process flow

This future state "to-be" process flow provides us a smooth flow of steps from start to finish with key prioritized requirements planned for phase 1 of the project roadmap. More functions and automation will be added in later phases of the project.

Benefits of creating process flows

There are many benefits of creating process flows. Let us list some of the key benefits of a good process flow diagram:

- Users can understand the complete picture if it's represented visually in a logically sequenced step
- Since the steps are connected, we can identify interlinking between cross-functional tasks
- Identify redundant tasks and eliminate them
- Identify duplicate steps and fine-tune the process
- Helps us identify gaps and opportunities
- Shows us areas for improvement by identifying bottlenecks in the process

- Serves as a document for new and existing team members to understand the process and their contribution to the process

- Provides artifacts for the technical team so that they can use them for solution design and technical development

- Provides artifacts for the testing team so that they can use them for developing test scripts and creating test scenarios

- These are made available in training manuals so that users get a visual of the end-to-end process

- The process flow can be used to aid requirement traceability

Here, I have listed a few process flow models that I often use and found to be very useful and effective. There are many other models available to capture process flows; it is best to use the one you are most comfortable with:

- **Business Process Modeling Notation (BPMN)**: This is used to model business processes and is more advanced than Flow Charts. BPMN is a flowchart method that allows teams to graphically capture and document business process flows and provide a clear view of a specific process in sequential steps from start to finish. BPMN flows enable us to clarify communication between different project stakeholders and aid in business process improvements.

- **Flow charts**: This is similar to BPMN but less restrictive in terms of notation. It is useful for less complex flows. A flowchart is a diagram that graphically represents a process in a sequence of steps and decision-making points. Using a flowchart, we can communicate complex processes in a clear, understandable format with our stakeholders, and also improve business processes.

- **Unified Modeling Language (UML) diagram**: This is used to model software systems but can be used for process modeling. UML is a general-purpose modeling language that defines a standard way to visualize the designed system. UML is useful for specifying, visualizing, developing, and documenting a software system. UML is like a blueprint and very useful for software developers during the design and development of software systems.

Summary

In this chapter, we started by learning how to develop the current state "as-is" process flow. We took help from key stakeholders and experts in their areas to develop a process flow in which everyone has a common understanding. We analyzed, elicited further, and identified gaps and opportunities. We took the list of prioritized requirements and mapped them to the current flow to derive the future state "to-be" process flow. In doing so, we identified opportunities to enhance the user experience by simplifying and automating processes.

Process flows are static diagrams, and they capture the essence of the business flow for a specific period. The "to-be" process flow we developed will be used as the current or "as-is" process flow for the next phase of the project. With good collaboration and by using the right tools and techniques as a business analyst, you will be able to create a great visual flow that helps stakeholders, end users, the technical team, and the testing team understand how the requirements are tied to the business process flows.

If you have never tried out process flows before, give them a try – you and your team will see immense benefits from all facets of the projects. As mentioned earlier, you do not need any fancy tools to get started. All you need is a whiteboard and a few colored markers – or even a few colored pens and paper.

In the next chapter, we will cover the steps and tools to document requirements in a **Business Requirements Document (BRD)**. Here, we will cover both user and product requirements capturing. We will also outline the details that need to be captured so that the technical team and quality team can understand and use this as the main document for the next phase of solution design, development, and QA testing project activities.

Questions

1. Recollect a few benefits of the current state process flow.
2. Process flows are snapshots of a process for a specific duration – True/False?

Further reading

- *Essential Business Process Modeling* by Michael Havey
- *Partner Relationship Management*: https://trailhead.salesforce.com/content/learn/modules/partner-relationship-management

5
Business Requirements Document

In the previous chapter, we learned about process flow diagrams. We started by developing the current state process flow and then refined the process by analyzing and identifying gaps and improvement opportunities. By effectively collaborating and using the right techniques, we can develop a process for the desired future state.

This chapter will discuss how to document requirements in a **Business Requirements Document (BRD)**. We will cover two types of business requirements – user and product. We will discuss functional requirements and non-functional requirements. We will review the level of detail to be captured in the BRD so that a business team, technical team, and quality team can understand the requirements in greater detail with a rationale so that they can address true needs during the solution design phase of a project.

We will be covering the following topics in this chapter:

- Reviewing the need for business requirements documentation
- Understanding user requirements and use cases
- Exploring functional and non-functional requirements
- Learning what level of details is sufficient
- Explaining a typical BRD and its key attributes
- Practical tips for success

By the end of this chapter, you will understand the importance of documenting a good BRD. Along the way, you explore different types of requirements, what they mean, and their relevance. You will get to know the key attributes of the requirements matrix and the structure of a BRD document.

Reviewing the need for business requirements documentation

A BRD is a very useful, beneficial, and valuable document for all project stakeholders, irrespective of the project methodology they use. When it comes to larger projects, we use a hybrid approach, where design and testing are done iteratively using the agile approach, whereas the rest of the phases fall under the waterfall model with some level of iteration to get maximum value. The BRD document details various aspects of the requirements so that you get the complete picture. If your project is 100% agile, you can skinny down the document and use only the requirements matrix document (covered in detail in the *Requirements matrix* section), which can serve as your product backlog. The BRD is your most important document for all your subsequent project deliverables. Your effort in documenting the BRD concisely, accurately, and clearly will help reduce issues manifold as the project progresses. For example, one incorrectly understood requirement can generate multiple defects during the testing phase or after post-production.

BRDs are used for recording business requirements relevant to your project implementation in a standardized format so that your business stakeholders and project, testing, training, and cross-functional teams can understand the business requirement very clearly without any ambiguity. The goal of the BRD is to document high-level business processes as they relate to detailed business requirements. First and foremost, the business stakeholder should be able to understand and agree to the requirements, and then we need to make sure of the following:

- The technical team gets enough details for them to start their solution design and technical development
- The QA team understands how to capture all possible scenarios for the test scripts
- The training team understands the documented requirements at a high level so that they can plan training activities
- The BRD can be used as a project artifact to support your project process
- The BRD can be used later in the project to create a requirements traceability matrix
- New stakeholders and project team members can get a complete idea about the functionality and scope of the requirements

> **Note**
>
> I would like to stress that the right level of documentation is very helpful for future functionality extensions. Let's say you did a few quarterly releases of agile projects and completed your roadmap. The team is disbanded, and team members move to different departments or different companies. Down the line, after 2 years, you plan to enhance the functionality. In Salesforce, for example, you have to enable a new and improved lighting framework and other new features, functions, and enhancements. Documenting details in the BRD will help the new project team members quickly and easily understand the scope of functionality implemented so far, thus saving time and resources.

Now that we know the importance and benefits of documenting business requirements, let's take a look at user requirements and use cases. These two terms are often used in traditional project management methodology.

Understanding user requirements and use cases

A user requirement describes the requirements from a user's perspective. What does the user need in simple non-technical terms?

In the past, traditional requirements used to place emphasis on the following:

- Capabilities, such as what a system can do

- Constraints, such as what a system cannot do (limitations)

These traditional requirements have evolved, and analysts started adding the "user" element to traditional requirements. This adds clarity to requirements by describing what a specific user role can do with a software system so that they can achieve their desired goals. For example, a sales analyst shall be able to create prospects or customers from the **Account Management** screen.

Use cases are users interfacing with a software system. These entail sets of steps between the user and the system. In a way, use cases are user requirements but captured in a little bit more detail in the form of steps. Use cases state user needs and ways they can interact with the system to achieve an objective:

- **Who**: The user role (actor)

- **What**: What the user wants to do (action, which includes steps and sequence to complete a task/process)

- **Why**: Why the user wants the desired goal (benefit)

- **How**: The system reaction (output, such as a success or failure message to user input)

We will discuss the use case steps before we document user requirements. Almost all the time, I observed stakeholders and project team members referring to user requirements as use cases. In this book, I will use user requirements and use cases interchangeably. In the end, we would like to capture the requirements that are easily understandable and digestible by all our stakeholders and project team members. At the same time, we try not to use technical jargon, systems, or solution details. On average, if your team captured requirements clearly and accurately, for the majority of the projects, a business analyst should be able to confidently walk through an approved and finalized list at the rate of ~10 requirements per hour with your stakeholders or technical team members.

The next step after understanding use cases and user requirements is to get into more detail about what these user requirements are made of. The user wants to do something, and the system should let the user perform certain steps (actions you can observe) easily and reliably (non-observable). We will discuss this in the next section.

Exploring functional and non-functional requirements

High-level business requirements translate to more detailed user requirements and these further evolve into system requirements. We can classify these system requirements into two main types called functional and non-functional. Let's review some of them in detail.

Functional requirements

Functional requirements describe a specific set of capabilities that a system must provide to users. They define a system or capabilities. These are the actions that users would like to perform so that they can achieve the desired and expected business needs. Functional requirements can be stated and captured using various tools and techniques we covered in the previous chapters. With good knowledge of a business area, underlying software and business analysis skills, and collaboration with knowledgeable stakeholders/SMEs, you should be able to capture these requirements accurately.

Let's look at a small sample of the common functional requirements:

- **Business rules**: These are the main business drivers for your organization. For example, discounts on quotes for customers are based on customer type and the total dollar amount.

- **Authentication**: User authentication is required to access the system. For example, all users accessing Salesforce applications can access Salesforce applications via SSO on the company network or via VPN.

- **Audit tracking**: As per compliance, a company mandate is to track field-level changes, such as who created/changed something and when. For example, the compliance department would like to track changes to opportunity name, amounts, owner, and stage changes.

- **Security**: Who can see what and from where? For example, different users can access a system based on assigned roles, profiles, and whitelisted IP addresses during the 9 AM to 5 PM user time zone.

- **Interfaces with internal and external systems**: No business runs on one system. On average, there is some kind of interfacing with around 6 to 10 systems. For example, in the financial service industry, a Salesforce CRM system can integrate with KYC systems, risk rating systems, Splunk, business objects, data warehouses, CPQ systems, SAP systems, and HR systems. Some complex implementations may have way more integrations.

- **Reports and dashboards**: You can add these as default functional requirements to all your implementations. You need tons of them. In the earlier days, we used to gather requirements for reports and dashboards, and the technical team or system analyst used to enable this for users as part of the project release. Now, we empower our users to create their reports. We provide training and guidance as needed. Still, we need to capture this as a requirement, as the technical team needs to make sure that all fields are available during reports and dashboard creation. For example, in Salesforce, we need to make sure relevant fields are added to custom report classes so that users creating reports have access to those fields.

Non-functional requirements

Non-functional requirements describe characteristics or quality attributes. These requirements are not obvious and need experience in the underlying technology to be able to capture them. Collaboration and involving technical team members such as technical leads, software developers, and solution architects can help in identifying and defining these requirements. Understanding functional needs accurately helps the team unearth hidden non-functional needs. Non-functional needs are extremely important for better user adoption and system usability. For example, a simplified **User Experience** (**UX**) does not mean removing some functions but rather keeping more features and automating steps for a user. This means your project team's goal is to hide all the complexities behind the scenes and implement a solution that is intuitive, quick to learn, and easy to use. This can be accomplished only if we can identify possible non-functional requirements. For every requirement, make sure to think through non-functional features associated with each functional requirement.

Let me give you a practical example so you can get a better idea. During one of my first Salesforce CRM releases a very long time ago, the functional requirement stated, "Sales analyst shall be able to create customer record from account screen." It looked pretty straightforward to implement. When our technical team started unit testing, we observed that the account page stretched four long pages on a regular desktop screen. Added to this, we had multiple validation rules that caused a lot of frustration, as we were unable to save the record unless all those fields were filled accurately. Even after filling in so many fields, the screen used to time out and all the data had to be rekeyed. Fortunately, our team learned from this and identified a few more functional and non-functional requirements where we could default values, automate processes, and limit fields for users to input. Imagine what could have happened if we had implemented this solution for end users. The lesson we learned was to always think about actions from a user's perspective and see how we can enable simplified technological solutions and help them focus on business, not on how technology works.

Let's look at a small sample of the common non-functional requirements:

- **Usability**: Is the functionality easy and intuitive to use from a user's perspective – for example, simplified screen navigation, guided screen flow, and being able to access from any browser/device?

- **Reliability**: The user should be able to trust the reliability of the system. For example, the user should be able to successfully save data and retrieve it later easily without any data loss.

- **Performance**: The user should experience good performance all the time. For example, screen refresh should not take more than a few milliseconds every time. It should be instantaneous and they should not have to wait.

- **Scalability**: Being able to scale an application – for example, adding more users or data without performance degradation. With a Salesforce CRM cloud application, this is never an issue, as the SaaS provider takes care of this.

- **Availability**: Availability of a system to users other than those scheduled and planned upgrades or maintenance activities.

- **Maintainability**: How easy it is to maintain an application after implementation – for example, can our existing production support team maintain bug fixes, and do they have the necessary training, skills, and access to project artifacts to understand user problems?

- **Data management**: Enable encryption for data at REST and in transit, periodic password recycling, and vaulting of non-human accounts, such as APIs, web service calls, and integration accounts.

We have covered only some of the system requirements to give you a general idea, and you may have many more that may apply to your project implementation. Now, let's explore and see the level of detail that needs to be captured for each of our requirements.

Learning what level of detail is sufficient

Requirements should be captured with sufficient detail in simple language, with business terminology as much as possible so that stakeholders, SMEs, and other business users can relate them to their everyday work. As well as its own culture, each organization has its own business language and acronym usage. This is the language you can see everyone using effortlessly, and it is very specific to your organization. Creating a document in its users' terminology will chime with their thinking process and understanding. You can use business terms and elaborate the requirements a little bit so that others can understand too. Do not make it too detailed and too lengthy; otherwise, no one will read it.

> **Note**
> To see what level of detail is sufficient, the first thing you should do is business analysis, and the project team should get conversant with business jargon. Unless you know these terms well, you can never understand a business user, let alone their needs. Make a glossary of all the business terms and socialize with the project team. Business stakeholders assume you are aware of these terms, and they continue to talk in that language whether you understand it or not, so be prepared.

You can capture requirements and details in tools approved by your organization. One of the tools I prefer to use is Jira. In this section, rather than discussing a specialized tool, let's go with Excel spreadsheets. We will document all our prioritized requirements in an Excel spreadsheet. You can call it a requirements matrix, product backlog, or list of approved requirements. It is essentially a list of all your approved prioritized list requirements. I prefer to call this a requirements matrix, and we capture each requirement with the following attributes in an Excel spreadsheet, later attaching this sheet to our BRD. Please make sure that you document BRD with enough details, even if you use agile methodology. No matter what people say, proper documentation matters, and this BRD is our opportunity to do so. This is the first important document/artifact that other teams and subsequent project phases utilize to bring life to a requirement. This is your business requirements blueprint.

Requirements matrix (prioritized product backlog)

Before we get to the BRD document, let's take a look at individual requirement attributes in a requirements matrix (or prioritized product backlog):

- **BRD ID (unique ID):** One good approach I have seen people use is grouping requirements by functionality or module. For example, account management starts with `Account001`, opportunity management with `Oppty001`, contact management with `Contact0001`, and so on. This way, team members will immediately know what module a requirement belongs to as well as how many requirements there are in each module.

- **Purpose:** The objective of a requirement.

- **Summary:** A requirement summary in simple terms.

- **Normal flow:** The most optimistic flow. This is what the user does to achieve their goal when no issues are encountered – a happy path.

- **Alternative flow:** If the user encounters issues, provide steps for them to take a different flow.

- **Exception flow:** In the event of an error, this will be the system response.

- **Business rule:** Capture business rules associated with a requirement. For example, a close date on an opportunity cannot be in the future, or to be able to close a deal successfully, a KYC process has to be approved for a customer account.

- **User actions:** The steps the users perform – for example, logging in to Salesforce, accessing the **Contact management** tab, clicking on **Create new records**, entering all the required fields, and successfully saving the record.

- **System response:** The system displaying a human-understandable success, error, or information message – for example, contact "Mr. Srini Munagavalasa" successfully created.

- **Category:** Identifying the requirement importance using your method of choice – MoSCoW, priority, or complexity.

- **Phase of project:** Whether a release is in its first phase, the second phase, and so on.

- **Documented date:** The date when a requirement is added to a matrix.

- **In/out scope:** Your prioritized list usually consists of approved in-scope items; in some cases, due to technical limitations or resource constraints, you can defer a few requirements to future releases. Here, you can tag the deferred ones as out of scope.

- **Comments:** Add any comments or details that add clarity to your requirement.

These are some of the key fields; add other fields as needed to your requirements matrix. These documents should be detailed enough but not too detailed. After completing it, read it assuming someone else prepared it, and see how you feel. Get it peer-reviewed and ask for at least a few suggestions to improve the matrix. Reviews provide you an opportunity to improve the requirement matrix and help you get it as accurately as possible before you can publish it to a broader group of users.

> **Note**
> If the technical team and training team members often consult you for clarification of the documented requirements from the requirements matrix, it means you did not capture the requirements clearly. Take time to revise and review them. If not, you will waste time clarifying these requirements to different teams again and again.

Explaining a typical business requirement document and its key attributes

In this section, we will look into the main sections of BRDs. I have outlined simplified documents that give an overall picture of the business requirements relevant to your project. If you do not have your project-specific standard templates, feel free to start with the one discussed here, keep adding sections as needed, and create a standard document for your projects.

The typical components of BRD are as follows. If your organization is mature, you may have your own **Project Management Office (PMO)** and **Center of Excellence (COE)**. This document is highly requested and may be mandated as part of your project documentation and for business requirements approval. Moreover, it has a higher purpose and serves as a starting point for the next phase of project activities, such as your solution design and functional design.

To give you a general idea of what constitutes a BRD, let's look at some of the following sections. Understanding various sections and their purpose will help you document your BRD accurately:

- **Introduction**:
  - **Project overview**: A brief business background for this project.
  - **Objectives**: What is expected from this project/release roadmap.
  - **Challenges**: The current challenges impacting the business. List inefficiencies and major pinpoints.
- **Project team members**: Everyone who will be directly or indirectly impacted by changes:
  - Stakeholders
  - SMEs

- Super-users
- Technical/training/DevOps team members

- **Project scope**:

  - **In scope**: Document core functions at a high level – for example, account management, opportunity management, campaign management, D&B Hoovers integration, DupeBlocker, and so on.

  - **Out of scope**: Highlight items out of scope for a specific release. They can be in scope for a future release. For example, quote/contract management, mobile capabilities, and Data REST encryptions are not in scope.

  - **Assumptions**: Specify your assumptions. For example, all end users are on Windows 10 and use either an Edge or Google Chrome browser.

  - **Constraints**: List limits or restrictions. For example, not hiring a solution architect on time may delay integrations.

  - **Issues/risks**: Things that may adversely impact a project – for example, low stakeholder engagement or requirements changing all the time.

- **Project roadmap**: Insert your roadmap for the projects. What functions are going in which release?

- **Current state analysis**: Add your "as-is" process flow. Highlight the pain points and constraints in the current way of doing things.

- **Proposed/desired future state requirements**:

  - **Future state flow**: Add your "to-be" process flow. Explain briefly your future state flow so that users get an idea of what they can expect.

  - **List of all requirements (business level)**: Refer to the requirements matrix. In addition to attaching, add a few lines of each of the following items. Some key high-level stakeholders may not have time to go through your requirements matrix. This provides them with key items that are being addressed as part of your release/project. Do not copy everything from the matrix here; just add a few most important items only:

    - **Functional requirements**: For example, account management with a 360-degree view of the customer, opportunity management with pipeline reporting and sales forecasting, or campaign management with HubSpot integration

    - **Nonfunctional requirements**: For example, a user shall be able to see all search results in less than 1 second, or a report refresh should not time out

    - **Regulatory and compliance requirements**: For example, a user should not be able to edit or delete closed-won opportunities

- **Reports and dashboards**: Document summarized reporting and dashboard requirements – for example, a pipeline report by industry verticals, a matrix report of all opportunities by business unit and stage, or a partner management dynamic dashboard

- **Interfaces**: Document a one-liner description of the interface in simple terms for business stakeholders to understand – for example, account integration with D&B Hoovers for data enrichment

- **Data requirements**:

  - List data conversions in scope and the respective templates to collect data from legacy systems. (Attach files here – one file per data load with instructions and a few rows of sample data.) The data migration process involves **extracting, transforming, and loading (ETL)** legacy data. This is one of the most critical project activities, which can jeopardize your whole project if not done accurately. During the functional design stage, we will capture more details on how to migrate master and transactional data in a usable format.

- **Reports and dashboards**: A sample mocked-up format of reports. Attach a sample of legacy reports and dashboards so that you have a minimum baseline of what a business needs, and try to improve upon it as much as possible. Also, utilize out-of-the-box Salesforce features such as scheduling reports and dashboards to groups of users.

- **Training requirements**: Training widely varies based on the project. If it is a completely new implementation, functionality-wise and software system-wise, then you need to spend extensive time planning, preparing, and facilitating training and creating training artifacts:

  - **Scope of training**: The number of users to be trained, time zones, training material requirements, meeting tools (such as Zoom, WebEx, and Teams), recorded training, and so on

  - **Knowledge articles**: Details about the functionality usage instruction for end users with screenshots

  - **Cheat sheets**: These are also called quick reference one-pagers

- **Stakeholder RACI matrix**: List a **Responsible, Accountable, Consulted, and Inform (RACI)** assignment matrix so that project team members know who needs to be contacted and communicated with.

- **Service Level Agreement (SLA)**: An SLA defines how a service shall be provided post-going live. If you have a separate production support team, you need to work with them on how SLAs are addressed. Defining and planning for an SLA from the start helps set expectations with end users. Also, make sure you have reporting metrics created to measure an SLA by week/month/quarter.

- **Glossary of terms**: Capture all your company, business, and project team lingo. All acronyms should be captured here, including the most obvious ones.

- **Appendix**: All artifacts related to business requirements are to be captured here. If you are using a document management system, refer to the document via the link from here rather than attaching documents.

- **Revision history/version management**: Like any good document, capture who did what, when, and why here. Versioning helps team members easily identify and understand changes.

We have identified all key sections in a typical BRD, as needed, and tailored it by adding or removing parts of it to suit your initiatives. You may have to spend a good amount of time when you create a BRD for the first time. For subsequent releases on your project roadmap and other related projects, you can reuse most of the content from this BRD. Almost 75% of the content can be reused as-is. Investing time now will save time for your project team in the long run.

Let's review a few best practices so that you can be effective in your BRD creation.

Practical tips for success

Listed here are a few tips that are specifically useful during requirements documentation:

- **Collaboration**: You need to work with the technical lead, architects, lead developer, QA lead, and training team members to prepare this document. Their input is very much needed to capture various attributes, such as alternative flow and system response. This collaborative team will help to identify business context-related missed requirements. You need to adopt an iterative approach and need tight collaboration so that the team members are comfortable with what is documented. They are the main consumers of this document. Once the document is finalized and agreed upon by this team, socialize the final version with key stakeholders, walk them through it line by line, and get agreement and approval.

- **Visual artifacts**: Utilize any flow charts and screen mockups created during prior phases while documenting the BRD. This will help to keep the team focused on detailing each requirement.

- **Use simple language**: Use simple and complete sentences that all stakeholders, including the business users, are able to understand. Be generous and use business terms and acronyms as much as possible so that users can relate them to their daily business.

- **Documenting**: Invest time in structuring the document logically and clearly, and ensure it is peer-reviewed by SMEs. You and your team will refer to this artifact many times during your project roadmap. After baselining the document for your release, lock the document to prevent any further edits by team members.

You can make a BRD readable, engaging, and valuable if you can identify and collaborate with the right set of users, use the right visual artifacts, structure document flow logically, and use simple business language.

Summary

In this chapter, we reviewed various elements and components that are important for writing a good BRD. A BRD is a living document, and you learned how to complete the document with stakeholders and project team members iteratively to a point where it is clear and understood by all players. When you reach this stage, you take a baseline and version it. This version shall be your requirement scope for the release. Any changes requested from this point onward need to be compared to the baseline and need approval from the change control board before the BRD can be updated and versioned again. These new updated BRD versions shall go through the same process.

You have now gained insight and tips into what is needed for you to create a BRD that accurately describes the requirements that your stakeholder and project team members can understand.

In the next chapter, we will cover solution design aspects of system requirements. We will cover aspects where a designed solution is maintainable and scalable. We will also cover data-related requirements– the volume of data, legacy data, and data transformations. We take all these requirements, agree on a solution, and document all the steps with process flow in a functional document.

Questions

1. What are the main requirements that you capture in business requirements documents?

2. Why are transition requirements important? Can you think of a few examples?

3. Can you think of a few good examples where you can derive non-functional requirements with minimal effort?

Further reading

- *Use case* – Wikipedia: https://en.wikipedia.org/wiki/Use_case

Part 2:
Design, Development, and Testing – Iterative Cycles with Prototypes and Conference Room Pilots

In this part, you will learn about the next phase of the cycle – solution and technical design – where we will discuss prototyping, mock-ups, and wireframing the solution design, and use conference room pilots to socialize the output to stakeholders and SMEs and get their feedback iteratively, incorporating them in the solution. This part will help you learn tools, techniques, and methods that you can implement and incorporate to transform prioritized requirements into working system software. We will discuss various testing strategies and how to capture scenarios aligning to business requirement documents.

Some of the challenges that we see in most Salesforce projects will be discussed in this unit, along with methods to handle them.

We will address some of the key challenges faced during this phase:

- Stakeholders seeing the application for the first time after completion of the development phase rather than getting involved from the start

- Complicated design features and overloaded Salesforce user interfaces

- The ability to identify and understand elusive nonfunctional useability-related requirements that matter most for end user adoption

- Not planning or insufficient prototyping activities during different phases of projects
- Lacking conference room pilots and workshops
- Treating requirement traceability as a project artifact and not as an important tool for identifying test coverage

The following chapters will be covered under this part:

- *Chapter 6, Solution Design and Functional Document*
- *Chapter 7, Demonstrate Functionality Using Prototypes*
- *Chapter 8, Exploring Conference Room Pilots*
- *Chapter 9, Technical and Quality Testing*
- *Chapter 10, Requirements Traceability Matrix*

Solution Design and Functional Document

This chapter will cover different ways to identify functional and non-functional requirements using process flows during the solution design phase of the project. We will cover aspects where the designed solution is flexible, maintainable, and scalable. We will also cover data-related requirements such as the volume of data, legacy data, and data transformations. We will take all these aspects of the solution and document all the steps within a process flow in the functional document.

In this chapter, we will cover the following topics:

- Understanding solution design
- Identifying functional requirements
- Identifying non-functional requirements
- Reviewing data conversion requirements
- Understanding the functional requirements matrix
- Developing the function document
- Practical tips for success

By the end of this chapter, you will have gained firsthand experience with solution design aspects and in elaborating functional and non-functional requirements. You will have also learned to effectively analyze and enhance process flows and be able to identify and finish documenting the functional design document.

Understanding solution design

In the previous chapter, we successfully documented the business requirements in our **business requirements document** (**BRD**) in business-understandable and system-agnostic terminology. Solution design enables us to dissect high-level business requirements. In this section, we are going to refine them and deconstruct them into more granular details in the form of functional and non-functional requirements. These detailed requirements are documented in the solution design document, which is also called a **functional design document (FDD)** or a **functional specification document (FSD)**.

The following steps define the hierarchy of the flow of requirements:

1. We start with a prioritized list of business (stakeholder) requirements.

2. We further slice the requirements and add a little bit more clarity and details, and capture the requirements in a BRD. The approved BRD will contain our baseline requirements that have been approved and agreed upon by the stakeholders and project team members.

3. The next step is for us to add more granularity to the requirements to make sure we define requirements that the software system can fulfill. This is done via architectural design to define conceptual feasibility and then solution design to define feasible requirements.

4. Solution design requirements are documented in FD/FDD/FSD in technical terms so that the technical team can use this document to create a usable solution encompassing functional features and other system-related features. This allows the user to reliably and efficiently use the software features and functions.

There are two levels of solution design processes:

- High-level design, also called the solution architecture design process
- Low-level design, also called the component-level design process

The **solution architecture design process** is also known as a high-level solution design and provides potential and alternative solutions. This is when we decide which technology to utilize; for example, what type of middleware do we use for our interfaces? Is it on-premise or in the cloud?

We arrange all the functions in a logical sequence so that we can trace the process from start to finish. This process is iterative and the decomposition continues until we reach a stage where the solution has been analyzed, understood, defined, and agreed upon. At this point, the system is architecturally defined with all the potential requirements identified, which are verifiable, feasible, and consistent. We do our best within the constraints and project timelines, run this through a few iterations, and freeze the version and baseline. There may be a few open-ended functions that are not on the critical path, which can be added as assumptions and need to be determined soon.

> **Note**
> Always develop multiple conceptual flows; we need at least two alternative paths. This needs to be done at the same time we create the primary flow. We always need to do a *what-if* for every step in the flow. Each path should achieve the desired goal or objective.

The **component-level design process** is also known as a low-level solution design. The high-level BRD requirements are logically decomposed into the lowest-level functions. Each function is then analyzed for technical feasibility and technical aspects of the requirements such as availability, performance, and reliability to achieve an optimal solution. We use a logical decomposition process to improve our understanding of our technical requirements and their dependencies and relationships.

Solution design always starts with the conceptual flow that we created during the requirements gathering phase. We take this conceptual diagram and elaborate on it, along with the BRD requirements. During the initial iteration of solution design, we include and collaborate with the architects – the enterprise and solution domain, business analysts, technical leads, lead developers, and SMEs. We can use many tools to visualize and elaborate the conceptual flows into more granular steps in technical terms. During this phase, we consider the technology that shall be used while developing the solution design. An experienced domain expert will be able to identify most of the non-functional requirements and confirm or clarify the feasibility of the functional steps in the flow diagrams. We will discuss this in more depth by covering real-world scenarios. There, we will identify the hidden functional and non-functional requirements.

> **Note**
>
> There is no such thing as a perfect solution. With constraints on time, resources, and technology, the best we can do is come up with an optimal solution. Based on the complexity and criticality, we can use process flows and prototype techniques to gain more understanding and keep refining the solution design until we reach an optimal solution. This optimal solution approach has to be agreed upon and approved by key stakeholders. During development, design thinking helps us evaluate our development work, fine-tune the solutions, and make it even more optimal and ready for implementation by our technical team.

During the solution design phase, we identify functional and non-functional process flow steps. In the next section, I will walk you through a simplified practical real-life process flow and discuss how to identify new process steps.

Identifying functional requirements

We reviewed functional requirements at a high level in the previous chapter. We analyze these requirements from a technical perspective during the solution design phase and capture hidden and elusive requirements. These requirements are functional but not obvious to business users, without which we cannot enable the desired functionality effectively – for example, reducing redundant steps by automating certain processes.

Let's take a look at a realistic scenario. I have simplified very complex scenarios for the sake of clarity and understanding.

In terms of the BRD requirements, the following are the key ones; they are interdependent:

- Users shall be able to create customer records and be able to see products entitled by the customer based on the customer attributes industry, segmentation, and route to market

- Users shall be able to adjust entitled products by adding or removing certain products from the customer record

- Users shall be able to create opportunities and see all entitled products that have been added to the opportunity record from the customer record

The process flow is for opportunity product alignment, but we have to review these three business requirements as they are interdependent. If we don't align the products to the account record accurately, automatically adding products to the opportunity is not possible.

Take a look at the following diagram:

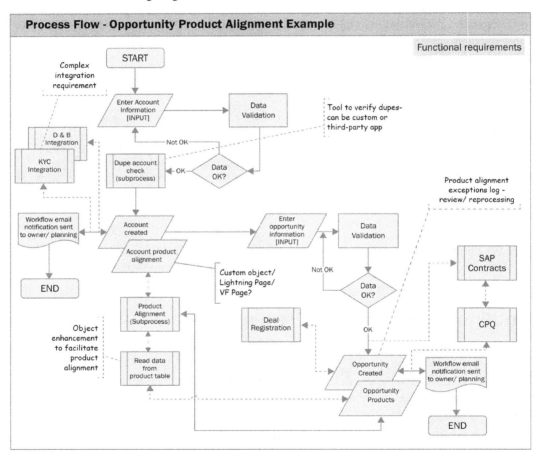

Figure 6.1 – Process flow – opportunity product alignment example (functional)

The process starts with a user (Sales Manager) creating an account record. We will try to keep the flow charts system-agnostic. Since we already know that our software system is Salesforce, I used Salesforce-specific terminology so that we can identify system-specific requirements.

Let's walk through the process flow from start to finish:

1. The user enters the necessary account information and saves the records. Then, the user inputs all the required fields and other optional fields as needed. A good practice is to input as many fields as possible since this helps other users have a complete understanding of the record.

2. The system validates the data input values. Here, we verify the business rules in the form of validation rules and prompt users with appropriate user-friendly messages.

3. Any validation errors that occur will prompt the user to correct the data input; for example, the KYC number should be 10 characters for US users and 12 characters for UK users.

4. If the data check is good, the system triggers a dupe blocker check and flags if the record is a duplicate. For example, if the user inputs a duplicate account name, then the system lists the duplicate value so that the user can navigate to the existing record and continue with the next step – that is, opportunity creation.

5. After creating the account, the product alignment sub-process kicks in and queries data from the product object. Products are added as per the business logic based on the customer attributes industry, segmentation, and route to market. The product alignment process is another complex flow on its own and in our scenario, we assume that we can align the products without any issues.

6. On successful account record creation, a workflow email notification is sent to the account owner and the planning team stating that the account record has been successfully created (another business rule). Based on how you configure workflows, you will be able to generate an automated notification with a link to the account record.

7. The user verifies that the products have been successfully added to the Account object. The product alignment object is a custom page/screen and lets the user manage multiple products on a single screen.

8. The next step is to create an opportunity record and let the system auto-create opportunity products. In this case, the user (the Account Manager or the Deal team member) creates an opportunity record.

9. The user inputs the relevant required and optional fields and saves the record. On saving, the system validates it. If no issues are found, it creates an opportunity record.

10. On saving, the system reads the product alignment from the account object and creates opportunity product line items. There can be one or more opportunity product records based on product alignment on the Account record.

11. Users shall be able to verify and, as needed, delete or add other products. Note that opportunity products shall be created automatically on new opportunities. Existing opportunities shall not be impacted during updates to the opportunity record.

12. A formatted workflow email is sent to the opportunity owner and the planning team with opportunity details and opportunity URL links.

13. The opportunity creation process ends. To simplify this process, I excluded steps such as opportunity edit, delete, and other exception steps on purpose.

14. Other integrations are possible, such as D&B, KYC, CPQ, SAP, and Deal Registration. I added them as dotted boxes to give you a general idea of how complex this can get.

It takes about three iterations to create and agree on this process flow. We refine each iteration based on the feedback. The more the team collaboratively discusses the flow steps in detail, the better we will be able to identify the gaps and missed steps.

Imagine what would happen if you had just one session with a key player and you, as a Business Analyst, presented this and got an agreement without getting any feedback. What if, at each step, the flow breaks after you deploy this to production? Without accurate process flows and being able to understand every stated and unstated requirement, can this be fixed by the support team after the project team has been disbanded? I will leave this to your imagination.

Now, let's take this through a few more iterations and collaborative workshops/CRPs with our key team members. We must question each step and see where it can go wrong and how we can make it better:

- How do we do de-dupe? Can custom code fulfill this requirement? Or can we use any available third-party tool? Who will be ultimately responsible for the data?

- Where do we capture the product alignment data? Can the user view and manage all the products on a simple screen? Do we need to account for additional development work?

- When products are added as opportunity products based on alignment, what if a record fails? How does the user fix the data? Do they add it manually or is there a way to capture the data and reprocess it automatically?

- To be able to convert account records from qualifying a lead to converting them into a customer record, customer KYC has to be completed and a KYC ID needs to be assigned to the KYC system. To enable this, do we need to build an interface or a web service call for the Salesforce system?

- Have alternative flows or options (including manual processes) been defined?

I am sure that if you review the process flow carefully, you will certainly find a few more requirements. Take a look and see if you can find two or three more. We try our best to identify all possible steps within the project's allotted time and available resources.

> **Note**
> Our goal is to identify all technical requirements to fulfill the business needs. How and when we implement them will come during the project roadmap. They can be staggered in releases; all core functions with some level of manual workaround should start within the first release and we must keep automating as we progress through future releases. We must lay out the end-to-end workflow so that users can get from point A to point B in the best possible way.

Next, let's review the same process flow and see if we can find any gaps concerning non-functional requirements.

Identifying non-functional requirements

Non-functional requirements specify the quality attributes of the underlying system. They are not easy to capture and not always obvious. Many of the non-functional requirements come to light only during the testing phase and especially during regression/load/stress testing. The objective of these requirements is to enable the sustained availability, reliability, and performance of the software. They help you ensure a good user experience and ease of system usage.

Take a look at the following diagram:

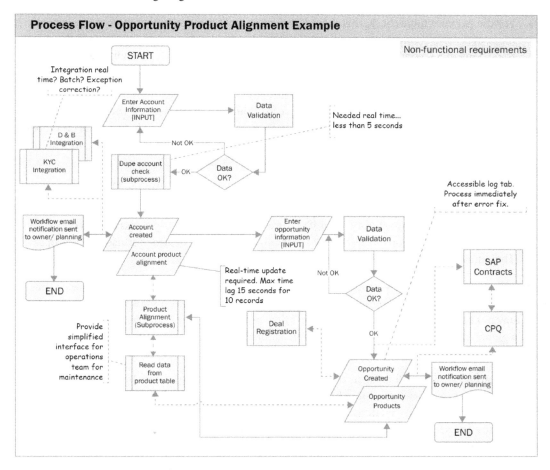

Figure 6.2 – Process flow – opportunity product alignment example (non-functional)

It gets easier to identify non-functional requirements if you draw out a flow chart and analyze it from start to end. At each step, we must analyze the non-functional aspects of every step in the flow for performance (the response time during peak usage), reliability (whether it's reliable on mobile devices), availability (whether the system is available 99.9% of the time), and so on. Detailed collaborative sessions with multiple iterations shall yield a good set of all possible non-functional requirements. Let's list a few here:

- What type of integration do we build with the KYC system (and integration with other systems such as CPQ and SAP)? Do we need it in real time or can it be a batch job? In this case, it may make more sense to have a batch job as the KYC process takes more time since the customer needs to be vetted and approved by multiple parties. In other instances, such as sending data to SAP contacts or the CPQ system, it makes sense to have a real-time call.

- For the Account dupe check, this should be done in real time, and it needs to happen instantly. Since every requirement needs to have quantifiable measurements, let's say we need the check to be done in 5 seconds. How about using a vendor app? If so, can the vendor app perform the check quicker than 5 seconds?

- How many product alignment records can be associated with Account records? There will be performance issues if there are too many records and usability issues if there are too many products (the user has to scroll through multiple pages, which may be a bigger issue on mobile devices). We need to capture this requirement and quantify the measure. Let's say that the system shall render 10 product alignment records in 15 seconds.

- We need to capture a way for the operations team to maintain the product table with product alignment attributes from the Account record.

- Upon creating the opportunity, what if the product alignment sub-process fails to create one or more product opportunities? What mechanism should we provide for users to reprocess? The same may be the case with account product alignment.

Hopefully, you can find a few more requirements if you review the flow again. Some of these non-functional requirements may vary based on what software system you implement. Also, some of them may not be obvious from a BRD or process flow perspective. For example, let's say that we are doing a global implementation – do we need translations? This will be a significant amount of work as screen fields, reports, workflows, and so on need to be translated to user locale-specific language.

Here, you can see how easy it is for us to capture these invisible requirements by exposing them on a simple process flow chart. Also, these flows are easy to understand for the team members and help them collaborate better. Start small with a conceptual flow and keep building it iteratively. If you plan and facilitate a few sessions well with the right set of participants, I am sure your team can reflect the business process and create optimized flow charts.

We can summarize both the functional and non-functional requirements into a single flow, as shown in *Figure 6.3*. Some team members like them to be separate as it is easy for them to understand functional versus non-functional requirements separately. Other team members prefer to add them to a single view. Pick the one that best suits you and your team:

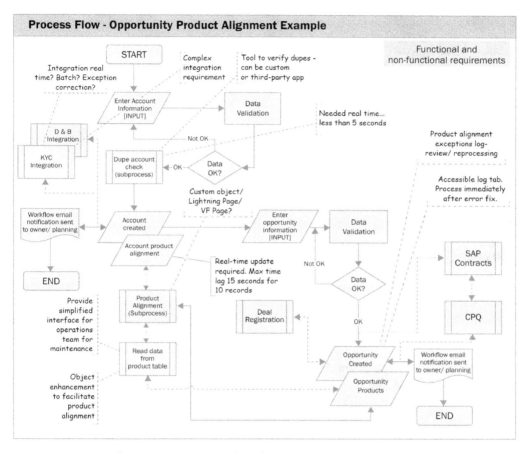

Figure 6.3 – Process flow – opportunity product alignment example (functional and non-functional)

With the aid of process flows, we can capture functional and non-functional process steps. Process-wise, the flow works well when the user creates new transactions (records). Does the functionality work with legacy data without any issues? This is seldom true and we need to consider migrating existing data from legacy systems. These requirements are not obvious in a process flow, so we need to make sure that we capture these requirements. Let's review them.

Reviewing data conversion requirements

Another important set of overlooked requirements is data conversion requirements. I have seen many projects that do an excellent job of enabling new functionality with a great-looking user interface, automations, workflows, reports, and so on, but they missed one very important requirement related to legacy data. Users can only use great features and functions if they can easily access their existing legacy data in the new system in a usable format. These data requirements fall under functional and non-functional requirements.

Some key tasks that you need to think through while capturing data requirements are as follows:

- The scope of the legacy data to be converted; for example, data sources, volumes, and history data.
- Map the data from legacy values to new values.
- Scrub the legacy data so that it can be extracted before it's converted; for example, for dedupe, completeness, and accuracy purposes.
- Dependencies between different tables/objects. Data needs to stick to the same dependencies in the target system to be usable.
- Define your **Extract, Transform, and Load** (ETL) processes.

Now, it's time for us to document what have we identified so far. We will document these newly identified requirements in a functional requirement matrix.

Understanding the functional requirements matrix

The functional requirements matrix captures more granular details and elaborated functional decomposition requirements. For each BRD requirement, we will add more granularity, which may result in multiple functional requirements for each BRD requirement. We take the business requirement matrix and add additional columns to capture the checklist fields for other teams – for example, for the development team to check for requirement completeness, feasibility, and so on and for the testing team to check for requirement clarity, testability, and so on. One important column that sits next to the BRD summary is the FD summary. It spells out the description in more detail so that the development and testing teams can get more clarity and details about the requirement. Feel free to use technical jargon so that the team developing the functionality is more comfortable. You do not need to make this functional requirement matrix too complex. Reuse the BRD and add a few more fields as appropriate for your project releases. For better clarity, add functional requirements to one tab and non-functional requirements to the next tab. This will add more clarity for developers and testers. If you prefer, you can combine both into one Excel sheet.

> **Note**
>
> Every requirement in the functional requirement matrix should reference at least one business requirement. Also, every business requirement should map to at least one functional requirement. If not, make sure you identify the redundant (a requirement in FDM but not in BRD) or gaps/ missed (a requirement in BRD but not in FDM) functional requirements.

Developing the function document

By collaboratively reviewing and developing the process flow charts, we were able to take each BRD requirement and further subdivide them into one or more functional and non-functional requirements. Each BRD item can be split into multiple functional and non-functional requirements, which the developers can use to build and unit test the sub-system or component.

Let's take a look at the functional specification document (or functional design document):

- **Introduction**: Provide a brief introduction of the project:

    - The purpose and core functionality that is being addressed

    - What business needs and objectives are served

    - Business units/countries impacted

    - Other projects directly or indirectly associated

    - Project stakeholders and project team members

    - User roles and profiles

- **Project approach**: A project management approach defines your team's mindset on how to run the projects. It depends on the project characteristics such as size, scope, and team dynamics. Based on the need of your software project, you may have to pick the right approach. It can be a traditional waterfall (plan-based), incremental (adaptive), or a mix of both:

    - **Methodology**: Project methodologies such as waterfall, agile, hybrid, or any other methodology mandated by your PMO

    - **Conventions and standards**: Project and Center of Excellence standards

- **Assumptions**: List all assumptions. For example, you can explicitly state the software system you plan to use. As an example, you can have Salesforce as the core CRM system, D&B Hoover for data enrichment, CPQ for pricing and quoting, and so on.

- **Constraints**: What are the constraints that may impact the project? This can include the budget, aggressive timelines, technical resource availability, conflicting projects, and integrations.

- **System landscape**: Briefly describe the new systems and their main features. It will be very helpful if the system's architectural diagram is added here:

    - **System impacted**: What systems are potentially impacted due to this release or project roadmap? Examples include SAP-OTC, CPQ, and KYC.

    - **System diagram**: Add the system diagrams that we created earlier, including the current flow, future state flow, and process flows.

- **Business workflow**: List all the workflows that are exiting, as well as the new ones that have been planned as a part of this release. For example, you could add a workflow that auto-creates products on an account based on product alignment.

- **Schemas/data flow diagram (DFD)/ERD**: Insert the schemas/DFDs that capture how the data flows so that the developer and tester can understand them clearly and plan and execute their development work:

  - Objects

  - Data field attributes

  - Data dictionary

  - Relationships

  - And more

- **Functional and non-functional requirements**:

  - Functional requirements matrix (BRD matrix expanded)

  - UI layout

- **Reporting requirements**: List all the reporting requirements, including the ones that need to be migrated from the legacy system (if any). This is to ensure that the specific fields that are created are accessible during reporting.

- **Interface requirements**: List all the interface requirements; for example, if they are real-time or batch. If a batch process is being used, then what will the frequency be, and what will the data volume be (full volume or only the delta changes)?

- **Standards**: Standards used during the development phase such as naming conventions, coding formats (including commenting code and code coverage), and reporting formats.

- **Disaster recovery plan**: List the disaster recovery plan and steps to be taken in case a system outage occurs. What will the business continuity plan be in terms of roles, responsibilities, and communication procedures? The plan should include data loss scenarios; if data loss occurs, then what is the plan to recover the data?

- **Appendix**: Add any relevant documents that help the technical team, such as your BRD, any conceptual flows, business presentations with key stakeholders, business plan, and so on. Add them as links or attachments.

- **Acronyms and abbreviations**: Company and technology-specific acronyms that are used in this document.

This is a comprehensive list of key sections in functional documents. As needed, add other relevant sections that you think add value to your implementation. Similar to BRD, you review this with technical and testing leads and SMEs, get agreement and approval from all, and lock this document. You should share this document with business SMEs and stakeholders so that they can review and provide input. However, their approval may be optional. This baseline version shall be your starting document for subsequent releases on your roadmap.

Practical tips for success

The following are a few tips that are specifically useful during solution design and functional documentation:

- The complete business process from end to end by function. For example, let's say you have three functions – Account Management, Campaign Management, and Quote Management. Here, you should use three end-to-end process flows.

- Capture all the steps, manual or automated. Remember, process flows are system agnostic and not all steps can be automated in one release. A manual process in one release can be an automated process in a future release.

- Create process flows with input from key team members. Incorporate feedback, finalize the flow, and get agreement from this core team. All members should be on board with the overall solution design before actual development work is started.

- The functional document is the main point of reference document for the technical and testing teams. Make sure enough details are captured, if possible, in technical terms.

- The functional document should address the **user interface** (**UI**) and usability of the application for better user adoption. As needed, it will be beneficial to mock up the screen's navigation, look, and feel.

- Address scalability requirements. If the data volumes are going to grow exponentially, the technical team needs to consider this during technical development.

- Another important aspect to consider is the performance of custom code or complex components on the page layout. For example, the product alignment page displays all the products on one page on the account record.

- How well is any system or data exception handled and logged?

- Plan the security aspects from the start. This includes a user's access based on location, time zone, IP restrictions, MFA, encryption, and so on.

- Doing functional document peer reviews before getting it signed off helps make it a complete document. Experts with knowledge in that area can provide valuable feedback, help iron out any open issues, and provide more clarity on how to document the requirements.

Now that we've covered some practical tips for success, let's summarize this chapter.

Summary

As projects grow in size and complexity, we need to make sure that we plan and allocate time and a budget for the solution architecture and solution design aspects during the design phase of the project. We can identify all the solution components and subcomponents by decomposing high-level functional requirements.

In this chapter, we learned about the solution design tasks, where we perform architectural design to identify all the steps in the process conceptually. Then, we learned about the functional and non-functional requirements with the help of process flows. Using this new knowledge of process flows, we captured the requirements in the functional requirement matrix. In the end, we reviewed a typical functional document and reviewed various important sections of the design document so that technical and testing teams can understand and use this as a baseline document for the next stage of the project.

In the next chapter, we will cover how to mock up quick semi-working solutions that we can demonstrate to stakeholders and team members and get early feedback on. We will also discuss the benefits of prototyping, conducting, and capturing the prototype by collaborating with the right stakeholders and team members.

Questions

1. State a few benefits of the functional document to your technical and testing teams.
2. What are the three main artifacts you may find useful during the solution design phase of your project?
3. List three key participants whose input is required that you need to involve during the solution design phase.

Further reading

*   *Salesforce Architect's Handbook: A Comprehensive End-to-End Solutions Guide*, by Dipanker Jyoti and James A. Hutcherson
*   *Becoming a Salesforce Certified Technical Architect: Prepare for the review board by practicing example-led architectural strategies and best practices*, by Tameem Bahri

7

Demonstrate Functionality Using Prototypes

In the previous chapter, we discussed solution design for our business requirements and documented functional and non-functional requirements in a functional design document utilizing process flow. We will take these requirements to the next level where we will prototype the functionality and demonstrate the functional look and feel, navigation, and **user interface** (**UI**).

In this chapter, we will cover demonstrating functionality aspects of how to translate the functional specification into a visual working model. We will cover how to mock up quick static or semi-working solutions that we can demonstrate to stakeholders and team members. During this phase, team members will be able to see a visual of the requirements and get an opportunity to ideate, collaborate, discuss challenges and workarounds, and continuously provide feedback.

We will be covering the following topics in detail:

- The need for prototyping and its categories
- Prototype stages
- What and how do you prototype?
- Tools to document prototyping
- The benefits of prototyping
- Practical tips for success

By the end of the chapter, you will have gained knowledge and understood the importance of prototyping activities. You will also learn about how you can plan and develop a good prototype that will avoid surprises at a later phase and get a consensus on the solution design aspect of the requirements.

The need for prototyping and its categories

A prototype is a mock-up, or a model, of an idea based on the business needs that team members can develop, interact with, and provide feedback on. A prototype can just be a static model or can be a limited functionality model and provide a way to visualize the proposed design solution beforehand. This idea is developed iteratively and organically with input and feedback from key team members and helps us move in the right direction. Building and socializing prototypes helps us see abstract ideas in a solid form where users can visualize them, concur, and confirm or reject them. We basically get all the associated team members on the same page and a greater understanding of the idea can be put into action. In some cases, the user who defined the business need or requirement may not really want the prototype solution at all or may want it to be different. Prototyping an activity responds to actual user needs by helping the users understand and see their own needs firsthand.

Categories of prototype

We can use prototypes to test both functional and non-functional solution aspects such as usability, scalability, and performance to a certain extent. I mostly focus on business requirement prototypes and UI and usability prototypes. Cloud application performance and capabilities are taken care of by the SaaS providers and I will let this be run by the QA team doing regression and stress testing:

- **Requirements**: Handled during elicitation to understand and demonstrate business processes.

- **User interaction and usability**: Handled during the design phase to define and demonstrate its look and feel, interface design, usability, and navigation.

- **Performance**: Handled during the end of the design phase and the start of the build phase to predict system performance with concurrent users. This prototype is mostly aimed at technical teams to prove the non-functional requirements and design the technical aspects accordingly to mitigate any constraints.

- **Capability**: Handled during the design phase to make sure that the underlying software can handle the proposed design.

Let's look at a simplified example: users would like to manage customer business plans where they can capture customer information, key contact information, product information, quarterly business plans, and opportunity forecasts. This form is filled out collaboratively by the sales team and customer team members.

So, where do you start? Currently, business users use Word document templates to capture customer business plans and collaborate on these documents via email.

What do we do? We have multiple options, and for simplicity reasons, we will explore two scenarios:

- **Scenario 1**: Take the Word document template and mirror it field by field in the target system, running over multiple pages. In this scenario, the user experience is somewhat inefficient and ineffective, but at least the business plan has a home.

- **Scenario 2**: How about redesigning the complete user experience and the UI and making it more fun and enjoyable for your business users and customers? We do not know whether our users like this design yet and we do not have the time, money, or resources to create this experience in the system. This is when prototyping comes in handy. We do a quick mockup of the UI and the experience on paper (or any tool of your choice), mapping all the user needs and thinking it through in their shoes. Your team will have to create multiple variants of the prototype, socialize with key team members, and iteratively enhance it until it is agreeable and acceptable to your business users.

The outcome of the second scenario is displayed in *Figure 7.1*:

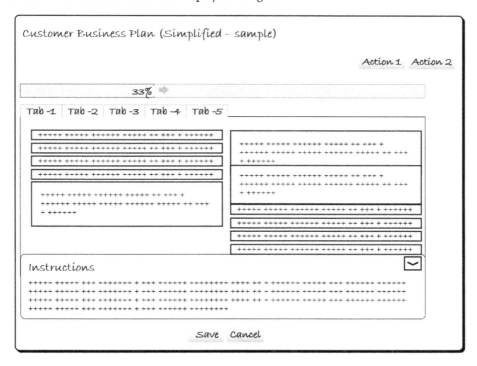

Figure 7.1 – A simplified sample wireframe

Let us explore each element on the screen:

1. We added tabs to capture the data for each of the functional elements. Users can navigate to each specific functional element by just clicking on the respective tab, rather than scrolling a few pages down:

    - Customer information

    - Key contact information

- Product information
- Quarterly business plans
- Opportunity forecasts

2. We added boxes for screen elements – fields such as text, date, amount, and picklists. Do not make them too detailed in this initial phase.

3. We added a few action buttons where the users can save, edit, print, or clear the data on the screen.

4. We added a progress bar indicator above the tabs so that the user gets an idea of what percentage of the form is completed.

> **Note**
> We need to strike a balance between too little versus too much prototyping. Too little effort means business users may not care and too much is risky. It should be enough to add just a little bit more to create some excitement. As in our example, we added action buttons and a status bar.

When to do prototyping

So, at what phase of the project or when is the best time to do prototyping? Typically, I would say you make a prototype during the solution design phase. You start with a rough draft prototype and progressively elaborate it and finalize it by the time you conclude the design phase of the project.

There may have been instances where I made a few prototypes based on very high-level business plans and during elicitation. You can make a prototype this early to validate whether the idea is viable and technically feasible within the constraints of the project.

Let us look at one example from one of my early projects. The requirement was to develop a partner locator in which customers would be able to locate distributors, integrators, and technology partners by location and product type. When we implemented this as part of Salesforce **partner relationship management** (PRM), we did not have many AppExchange tools or other third-party tools, and we were one of the early implementors of PRM. After doing some serious research and analysis, we came up with multiple options and zoomed in on one of them where we took an unmanaged package and redeveloped it to fit our needs. We quickly enabled this in one of our sandboxes and tested this with a small set of partner users. This is a true working model, and we enabled this for five users and worked with them, incorporating their suggestions and feedback.

This prototype is functional in the simplest possible way without exception handling, automation, and integrations. After we got the go-ahead from these pilot users, we went ahead and did another random usability test with another set of users before we made it into a full-fledged working solution with all the functions, automation, and integrations for our global audience incrementally during three releases. This is a case where you develop a working model prototype, then use this for **proof of concept**, and eventually the working model. We used evolutionary prototyping techniques to enable the functionality by starting simple and adding more incrementally by getting feedback from key team members and business users.

> **Note**
>
> When integrating a complex unknown function, always implement it incrementally in a few releases. This approach helps you gauge whether the sponsor(s) would like to move forward and invest resources into the next release. You do not need to implement and deploy 100% functionality in the first release. Implement the core functions with some level of automation and let the real user use them. Gather usability metrics and any pain points, such as too much search result data or a page rendering too slowly, and solicit feedback from users of the tool. If the usability reports show too low usage, maybe you need to rethink your next steps. Assuming the usage looks encouraging, incorporate your findings and add more automated functions and features in your next release.

Prototype stages

Let us look at the three stages of software prototypes:

- **Low-fidelity**: Low-fidelity prototypes are used to elicit initial feedback or to check whether the idea makes sense at all. These are draft or scratch prototypes where your team quickly creates relatively less functional and more flexible prototypes. Based on the feedback, they can be changed quickly.

- **High-fidelity**: High-fidelity prototypes are more functional and less flexible. We start with low-fidelity ones, refine the idea based on the feedback, and enhance the prototype with more features and functions, thus making it more sophisticated and closely reflecting the proposed functional solution. High-fidelity prototypes are working models and can eventually be used to build the final solution.

- **Medium-fidelity**: A medium-fidelity prototype, as the name suggests, is in between the low- and high-fidelity prototypes. I listed this one last for a reason since I usually do my prototypes at this level. My rationale for this is to have enough confidence in my prototype that key stakeholders and end users are comforted by seeing some level of functionality. High-fidelity prototypes are exponentially expensive and time-consuming and not a popular option, as there is a risk that you may ditch the relevant approach or functionality. Medium fidelity offers just enough features and functions with a good level of flexibility to adjust. Again, "medium" is a broad spectrum, so adjust it based on the functionality your team wishes to prototype.

Prototypes help us improve requirement gathering, solution design, collaboration, technical development, quality testing, and training artifact creations. They enhance understanding between stakeholders, SMEs, end users, and project team members. This also aids us in improving the UI and user experience.

Prototypes are made at every stage of the project to get a better understanding and allow all the key team members involved during the planning, designing, development, testing, and training phases of the project to collaborate. Prototype activity can be simple or become very complex. Based on your project, you can decide on the level of prototyping you need to do.

There are two main types of prototypes:

- **Temporary or transient prototypes**: These are also called throwaway prototypes. Examples of this type include simple wireframing or mockups of screens. As with other project activities, prototyping is also iterative. Key stakeholders and project team members are involved as part of the workshop or conference room pilot and the team will work on developing and designing the prototype collaboratively.

- **Evolutionary prototypes**: These are working models that simulate real-life functions. They are incrementally improved based on feedback from key identified team members and users. We keep adding functions and features and ultimately evolve this into a working solution. Remember – this will not be fully functioning as per the business requirements. For prototyping, we enable functions and features, but most of the steps are not yet automated or tuned. You can take this prototype as a model and build the complete solution during the technical development phase where all features and functions are automated and integrated and the UI is designed and enhanced.

> **Note**
> The key steps involved in an evolutionary prototype are concept (idea), developing an initial prototype, socializing, refining it until it is acceptable, and locking it down in technical development.

Prototyping can be horizontal or vertical or both:

- The horizontal prototype helps with understanding and demonstrating the overall scope of the functionality at a high level, where we create the breadth of the solution developed before getting into granularity. It provides a broader view of the complete system in scope for the project. Utilized to capture high-level requirements.

- A vertical prototype evolves as we keep building functionality on one specific function. Each feature is added incrementally until the proposed solution is developed. This prototype elaborates specific functions of a system and helps capture detailed requirements. The vertical prototype handles backend functions such as sizing, security, and performance.

What and how do you prototype?

Prototyping does not come free and some project implementations do not like the idea of prototyping, as they think it is a sunk cost. The reason for this is that getting the right SMEs and knowledgeable team members is not always easy. Also, business stakeholders do not like to sign off on the design approach.

I encourage you to do prototyping for any new feature and function that is specific to your project. You do not need to use fancy tools to do prototyping. All you need is a pen and a sheet of paper (a whiteboard or a flip chart, or a stylus pen and a pad).

Consider the following aspects when doing prototyping:

- **What is the scope?**: Keep it very narrow, only including the core and critical functionality for a pilot business unit with backend simulations (no or minimal automation or integrations).

- **Low, medium, or high fidelity?**: Start with low and refine it to medium. High fidelity is needed only if you plan to incorporate this logic in your final solution. Get the buy-in from key stakeholders at various stages and not at the end.

- **How much functionality to prototype?**: Start small and incrementally add more. Start with the absolute core functions, making some level of incremental addition based on feedback. Make sure you don't demonstrate a bare skeleton to business users. They may reject it outright on this basis.

Let's review the steps so that you get an idea. As with all project activities, proper planning and communication are very critical.

1. Select the requirements that you plan to prototype from a prioritized and approved list of requirements from the business requirements document. We pick the ones that are complex and team members find difficult to visualize or grasp proposed solutions for.

2. For the requirements that you plan to prototype, create business scenarios for each of the functions or sets of functions. Scenarios should include one happy path where everything works perfectly and a few alternative paths where you may run into issues. You can refer to process flows to get the sequence of the flow. These scenarios can be a simple set of step-by-step instructions of functionality from start to end.

3. We add more details to the prototype to show how the proposed functionality works on the system. We can add page layouts designed in a logical sequence, enabling fields based on the previous fields' attributes and helping users navigate them seamlessly. We can also prototype the same pages on mobile devices and verify navigation there too. Note that mobile navigation will be completely different from desktop browser navigation for Salesforce.

4. The prototype model is shared among team members and refined based on feedback. This process is iterative and the core team needs to work in an agile mode so that we do the demo, get the feedback, incorporate the feedback, and redo the iterative process.

5. We continue to revise and enhance in an iterative loop to create a comprehensive, well-rounded prototype. The core team members should be very critical and willing to provide open and honest feedback.

6. This final prototype, after its approval, can be utilized for the next steps in the project in the development of a functional solution. Although we invested a good amount of time into prototype activities, we are paid back when the prototype is accepted. This will cut down the development time and the risk of businesses rejecting the solution is rather slim.

Let us look at a practical example.

Here's the business requirement (or use case): a user (a sales analyst or sales manager) wants to be able to create and manage account records. Based on the account attributes, relevant products are added to the account screen (refer to *Figures 6.1* and *6.2* in the previous chapter).

We start with a quick and easy low-fidelity prototype of this functionality by wireframing the screen layout. This can be done rather quickly in a few hours by collaborating with the right set of key stakeholders and technical team members. By the end of the session, we should be able to wireframe screen layout design for the account and product alignment, as shown in *Figures 7.2* and *7.3*. At this point, let us not worry about how it can be technically enabled. We need to find out exactly the best and most simplified way for the business to utilize the functionality. Try to get to the optimal design solution that the team can approve and agree on:

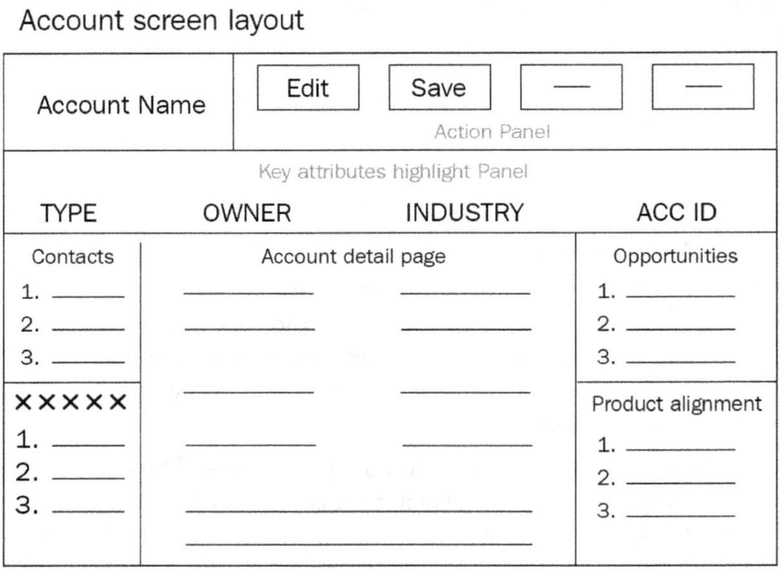

Account screen layout

Account Name	Edit	Save	—	—
		Action Panel		

Key attributes highlight Panel

TYPE	OWNER	INDUSTRY	ACC ID
Contacts	Account detail page		Opportunities
1. _____	_____	_____	1. _____
2. _____	_____	_____	2. _____
3. _____	_____	_____	3. _____
× × × × ×	_____	_____	Product alignment
1. _____	_____	_____	1. _____
2. _____	_____	_____	2. _____
3. _____	_____		3. _____

Figure 7.2 – The account screen layout wireframe

Here is a representation of the product alignment:

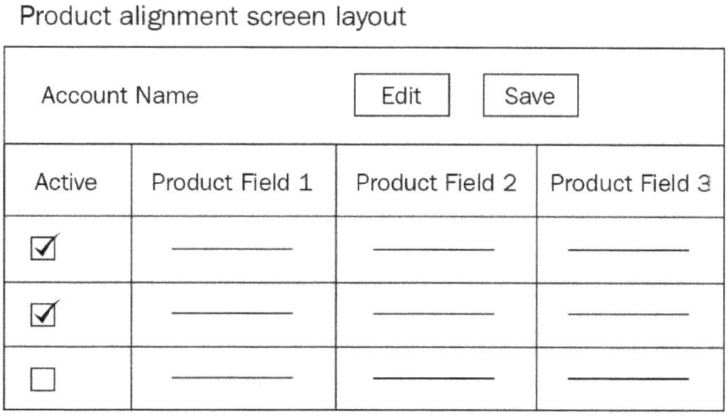

Product alignment screen layout

Account Name		Edit	Save	
Active	Product Field 1	Product Field 2	Product Field 3
☑	———	———	———
☑	———	———	———
☐	———	———	———

Figure 7.3 – Product alignment on the screen layout wireframe

The preceding wireframe clearly shows us the account screen layout and product alignment layout:

- A highlight panel displaying the key attributes of the account.

- Action buttons at the top (your business users may need them at the bottom too).

- Three-column 360-degree console view displaying the account details and related object details such as contacts, opportunities, and product alignment.

- From the account screen, the user can navigate to the product alignment screen (as we can see, the action button or link to navigate to product alignment is missing in *Figure 7.2* – make sure to capture the action button in your next iteration so that the user has a way to navigate to the product alignment screen).

- The product alignment screen lists all the products that are aligned to our account and the user can activate or deactivate products (again, we missed the action button for the user to be able to add new products, so make sure to incorporate this in the next iteration).

You can see how easy it is for us to get real-time feedback by visually depicting the business requirements in the form of a wireframe. This process helps us create designs in a short span of time with a common understanding across the entire project team.

Now that we have the okay from key business stakeholders in terms of the high-level UI design, let us add more details to this prototype. In this next level of prototyping, you need to involve your architecture, technical, and testing team members. Key business users and business SMEs need not be involved, as it involves more of a technical discussion that may include system capabilities and performance and capacity-related, non-functional requirements. We typically share this with key business users during the last iteration to get feedback on adding, removing, or rearranging fields or action buttons on the screen layout.

This is a good example of a horizontal prototype and provides a UI and user interaction rather than system functionality. Look at the following three figures (*Figure 7.4*, *Figure 7.5*, and *Figure 7.6*) and see if you can find opportunities to improve them in your next iteration.

A sample account screen layout view for the sales team is shown in *Figure 7.4*:

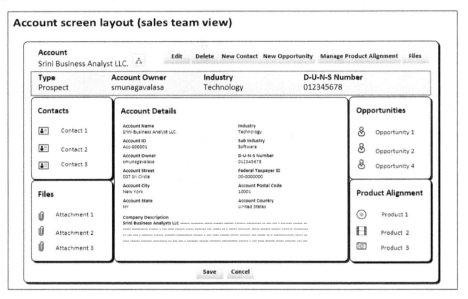

Figure 7.4 – A prototype of the account screen layout

A sample product alignment screen layout is shown in *Figure 7.5*:

Product alignment screen layout

Account
Srini Business Analyst LLC.   Edit   Delete

Active	Product Name	Product Family	Product ID
✓	Product Name-1	Product Family-1	Prd-100001
✓	Product Name-2	Product Family-2	Prd-100002
✓	Product Name-3	Product Family-3	Prd-100003
☐	Product Name-4	Product Family-3	Prd-100004

Save   Cancel

Figure 7.5 – A prototype of the product alignment screen layout

The following screen layout is a variant of the account screen layout. In this case, our service team needs completely different data attributes on the account screen. By rearranging fields and actions, we can create a completely different user experience for our service team. This will help us achieve high levels of user adoption.

Figure 7.6 – A prototype of the account screen layout (service team view)

As you can see for yourself, there's a considerable value you can create by prototyping and sharing this with the core team and getting their feedback to iteratively and progressively enhance the quality of the prototype and hence, the understanding of the proposed design solution.

Let us take a look at some of the tools that help us create these prototypes.

Tools to document prototyping

There are many excellent tools available on the market and you can pick the one you are most comfortable with. I prefer to use whiteboard and Visio to start my prototyping activities and then move into one of the sandbox software systems. I have listed a few of the ones I observed, tried, and used during my prototype activities and found very useful. I have heard there are other great tools too, so feel free to browse the web and try out a few trial versions:

- **Whiteboard/Flip chart/Visio**: This is the best and easiest when you are creating collaboratively with the team.

- **Balsamiq**: An easy-to-use and very effective tool. Best for wireframing and provides your team with the bigger picture.
- **Freehand**: A product from InVision. An efficient tool best for prototyping apps.
- **Adobe XD**: A feature-rich tool that requires some learning to use. An excellent tool for a **user experience prototype (UXP)** or **user interface prototype (UIP)**.
- **The software system itself**: When we try to prove the feature or function's feasibility, we can develop the feature in the Salesforce system itself. Remember this is only a prototype, so we do not need to prove 100% functionality.

The benefits of prototyping

Here are some key use cases to justify prototyping:

- Helps with the elicitation and clarification of business needs
- Identifies the missed steps or gaps in process tasks
- Identifies and refines redundant and duplicate tasks
- Aids in discovering design problems
- Involves end users from the start
- Allows us to identify complex functionality
- Gives stakeholders and SMEs a preview of the proposed solution
- Allows us to receive feedback from stakeholders and key end users
- Allows us to test and assess the feasibility and fitness of the solution
- Allows us to confirm and agree on a final design

Practical tips for success

Listed here are a few tips useful during the prototype phase:

- You need no specialized tool to start a prototype activity. This should not be a reason for you not to do prototypes. Simply use a whiteboard with markers.
- Prototype what is essential and not everything or anything. Time is limited, so choose functions and the level of functionality wisely.
- Consider user groups and how they interact with the software system. This brings in the most benefit to users – for example, sales analysts and service analysts can see a screen with different elements on it.

- Start with an inside-out approach where we prioritize the information and elements that are important to end users.

- Identify key participants during prototyping discussions and demos. Everyone needs to bring input to the table and strive to make it productive and useful.

- Make sure the technical team is involved and on board with the prototype design. They are the ones who will use them to build the final solution.

- Document the final version and share it with the team, along with other project artifacts. These versions will be very useful when the team enhances the functionality at a future date.

Prototyping helps team members see what direction they are heading in. Prototyping activities guide the team to see the potential future solution collaboratively and incrementally and in doing so, helps them course-correct any deficiencies and take advantage of any efficiencies.

Summary

Prototyping is extremely useful and helpful during software implementations. Prototypes help users and team members visualize or try out the functions and features, rather than interpreting and evaluating a design based on the descriptions in the business requirement documents. In addition, by involving the right stakeholders, we will receive feedback, and prototypes can be improved iteratively by adding or adjusting functionality. Prototypes keep the entire team on the same page. The end users will know what they are getting and developers will know what they are supposed to develop.

In this chapter, we discussed when and why prototyping is essential, along with the various stages and categories of prototyping. You also learned about horizontal and vertical prototyping and ample real-life examples of low-fidelity to high-fidelity prototyping. We concluded the chapter by learning the benefits of prototyping and a few practical tips that you can use for your project's success.

In the next chapter, we will cover the key aspects of conference room pilots where the product is demoed to a wider audience. You will learn how to facilitate a **Conference Room Pilot** (**CRP**) effectively, who to invite to these sessions, and how to keep the team focused on the agreed business requirements. You will also learn the key success factors and best practices that can help you during your own CRP sessions.

Questions

1. How is piloting different from prototyping?
2. When do you need horizontal prototyping and vertical prototyping?
3. Recall some of the prototyping techniques that we can use during prototyping.

Further reading

- *Agile Project and Service Management* (*Chapter 6, DSDM*) by O'Reilly

Exploring Conference Room Pilots

In the previous chapter, we discussed prototype activities and their benefits and came up with a solid design solution. You gained an in-depth understanding of various prototype stages and categories with practical examples. In addition to prototyping skills, you gained knowledge of the benefits of good prototypes and practical tips that can make you successful at creating prototypes.

In this chapter, you will learn how to showcase prototypes to a wider audience. We will see how **Conference Room Pilots (CRPs)** help us progress from individual requirements to proposed design solutions in the right direction without any surprises. We also will see how the testing team and the UAT team can benefit from the demos by helping them understand requirements as well as how they shape up into a functional working solution. This helps them come up with possible holistic scenarios and be able to validate the solution.

No project goes entirely smoothly. You will encounter surprises and that's what makes it more challenging and exciting. The earlier you encounter surprises, the better it will be for the team. This will give your team an opportunity to quickly reassess and understand the business needs better and align the project back in the right direction. This is where CRPs come to our rescue.

We will cover the following topics in this chapter:

- Understanding what CRPs are
- Exploring the timing and participants of CRPs
- Facilitating CRPs
- Managing scope creep during CRPs
- Reviewing the benefits of CRPs
- Practical tips for success

By the end of the chapter, you will have gained knowledge and understanding of the importance of CRPs. You will understand how CRPs can help identify and fine-tune functionality and usability and address any gaps in the requirements via a series of CRPs at critical junctures of the project. Concurrently, you will learn about the benefits that the testing team can derive from this activity.

Understanding what CRPs are

CRPs are workshops where key stakeholders, along with project team members, collaborate at various stages of projects to understand the business needs while transforming them into proposed business solutions. CRPs help stakeholders collaborate and see how their needs progress through each phase of the project, as well as being able to provide feedback. This helps users see what they are getting and keep the process transparent. Also, these CRP sessions help the technical team and testing team understand the needs better, so they will be able to deliver what the business truly wants.

Based on the complexity of the business requirements, the project team can decide when to do CRP and how often to do the CRP sessions. As a rule of thumb, I prefer to go with three CRP stages for a project with medium to high complexity and maybe a fourth one if the project is highly visible and critical or highly critical.

The four stages when we conduct the CRPs are as follows:

- **Scope CRP**: In this stage, we elaborate on the business needs/requirements. This is done during the plan/analyze phase of the project.

- **Design CRP**: In this stage, we connect various functional steps and integration points to understand the needs from a design perspective. This is done during the solution design phase of the project.

- **Build/development CRP**: In this phase, we actually show the users the actual functionality of the system. This is done during the technical development phase of the project.

- **Test CRP**: This is optional and recommended only for highly visible and very complex functionality. In this phase, we do a complete demo of the functionality, including any changes requested. This is to get all the stakeholders on the same page. Any suggestions or requests for changes are tabled and scoped for future release.

Based on the availability of time and resources, your project team can decide on how many CRPs they would like to do.

The CRPs we discuss in this chapter are critical project activities where the project team plans to do the following:

- Implement functionality on a new system, such as moving from old legacy systems into a totally new system. As an example, during our PRM implementation, we migrated partner data and functions from legacy systems and manual Excel sheets. Users do not know how to articulate their business needs. All they want is a system that they can use effectively.

- The project team implements totally brand-new functionality with a redesigned user interface and user experience. This functionality is very uncommon and your team may be one of the early adopters, such as implementing a partner locator.

- Your business users' needs are critical and highly visible. This is when you cannot go wrong at any cost, and you have dedicated business resources available for your project.

After understanding the various stages of CRPs, now it is time for us to explore and take a look at what point in the project and how often to facilitate the session. We will discuss what participants need to be invited to these sessions to make them valuable and productive.

Exploring the timing and participants of CRPs

For each of the CRP phases, plan to do two sessions. The first session is done mid-way through the project phase so that users get a chance to see how things are progressing. The second one is done at the end of the phase to get an agreement and approvals. The first session will usually be longer and can consist of 1 to 3 full-day sessions. The second session will usually be shorter. You do not need to plan exactly the same duration for all phases as it depends on your business needs. For example, if the requirements are vague, then the scoping CRPs can run for longer. Similarly, if the design is complex, then the design CRP needs to run for longer. In my case, when we did a PRM release, which is a high-priority company initiative, our first sessions lasted a week, where we invited key stakeholders from various regions to collocate in a full-day conference session. The second session we did was a hybrid model as it was too much for users to travel for in-person sessions.

Participant invitations will vary based on CRP phases. Since this session is time consuming, invite only stakeholders and project team members who can add value and are directly responsible for specific functions/capabilities.

A sample simplified schedule of the CRP is displayed in *Figure 8.1*. Below timeline, we have the project phases with a duration of about 6 weeks. Above the timeline, we have the CRPs planned approximately 10 days after the start of each phase and the second one just before ending the phase:

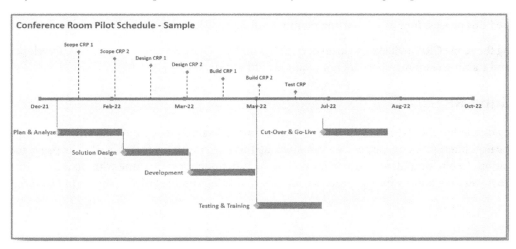

Figure 8.1 – CRP schedule (sample)

Let's discuss each CRP stage in detail in the next sections.

Scope CRP

During the scope CRP, we start with a whiteboard and progressively develop it into a simplified process flow where the team gets the opportunity to identify gaps and missing requirements. This is the phase where we develop the as-is and to-be process flows collaboratively with input from business users and SMEs. By the end of the scope CRP, our team comes up with a simplified process flow for one specific functionality in our project scope, as shown in *Figure 8.2*:

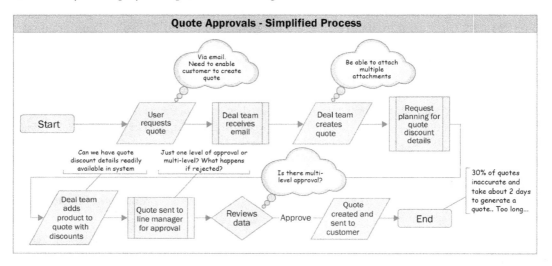

Figure 8.2 – Quote approvals – simplified process flow

We used this process flow as the starting point for our next CRP.

During the scope CRP, invite key stakeholders, SMEs, and only the core project team leads. Developer, QA, and training team members are not required at this stage.

Design CRP

During our design CRP, we refine the flow and create a more detailed process flow and screen mockups. For the user interface design aspect, we can mock up the screen with fields and design the pages and navigation. In our simplified example for one of the functionalities, we came with up a flow from start to finish for a quote approval process with each role doing specific tasks, as shown in *Figure 8.3*:

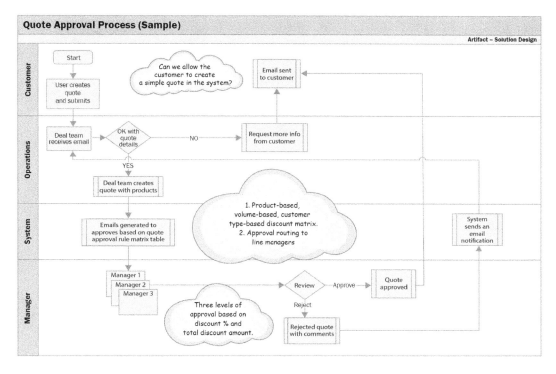

Figure 8.3 – Quote approval process

This process helps the stakeholders and the project team, especially our technical team, understand the process visually and be able to come up with all appropriate non-functional requirements.

During the design CRP, invite key stakeholders, SMEs, solution architects, technical architects, tech leads, and core project team members.

Build CRP

During the build CRP, our technical team started developing the functionality of the system. The demo done during the first build CRP will be more focused on the user interface and the happy path (or happy flow). After socializing and incorporating the input from participants, the technical team goes ahead and completes the fully functioning solution with all possible exceptions and error handling conditions. This fully baked product is demoed during the second build CRP. This is where the stakeholders and business users can view and get a feel for the proposed functionality of the system. The business users at this point usually tend to ask for more enhancements and it is up to the business analyst and project manager, along with the project sponsor, to manage and see what can be implemented now and what can be implemented later in a future release. A sample simplified solution for quote approval is shown in *Figure 8.4*. The figure displays the fully functional quote layout screen with action buttons such as **Create PDF**, **Submit for Approval**, and **Email Quote**:

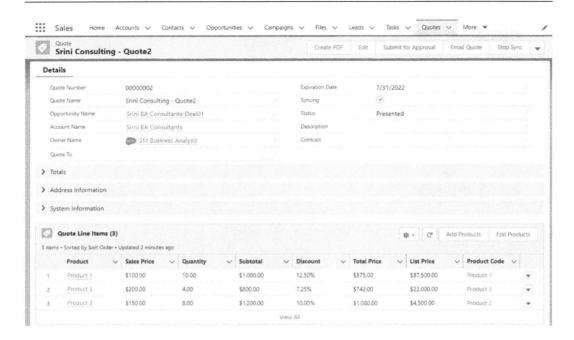

Figure 8.4 – Sample quote screen with fully functioning actions/buttons

During the build CRP, invite key stakeholders, SMEs, solution architects, technical architects, tech leads, dev team members, QA leads, and core project team members.

Test CRP

The last CRP is just before starting testing. We prep and load test data so that the user can use this data to test various scenarios. This one is optional as you can include this in the design CRP. Since this can be done via remote methods, I prefer to have this so that the business users doing UAT will have an opportunity to understand and see the functionality from end to end. This will result in fewer queries and waiting during the actual UAT phase. A sample screenshot with the output of the quote in PDF format is displayed in *Figure 8.5*:

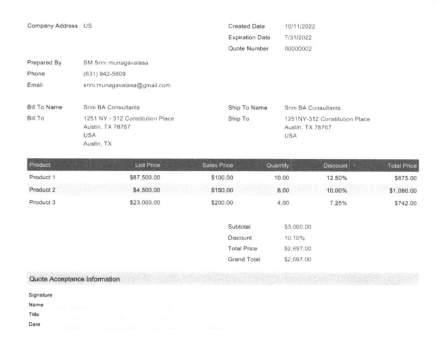

Figure 8.5 – Sample quote PDF page

During the test CRP, invite all team members as required. This can be just one session (about 2 to 4 hours) done hybrid (on-site and/or remote).

Spacing the sessions logically and planning them well in advance helps the team members get value out of the sessions. Their active participation and involvement keep everyone on the same page and leave no room for misunderstanding related to requirements, the designed solution, and, finally, the build.

> **Note**
> Try to keep session participants to approximately 20 team members. More than this will be excessive and may not be productive. Also, you do not need the same team members on all CRPs. Pick the ones that have the required knowledge and can add business value.

Facilitating CRPs

CRPs must be planned well in advance to provide an opportunity for the participants to make arrangements to attend these sessions. This means some participants may have to make travel arrangements and free up their calendars to be able to dedicate their attention and time to CRP sessions. To make this a rewarding experience for your participants, you need to ensure that the session is planned and executed efficiently and effectively.

Let us look at some of the important tasks that we can do to make CRP facilitation successful:

- Plan and create a CRP road map.

- Identify key participants of these CRP sessions: key stakeholders, SMEs, architects, and key project team members. Communicate with the participants after finalizing adding/removing team members before making a final list. Always keep a primary and secondary team member.

- Prepare a detailed agenda approximately 2 to 4 weeks in advance and communicate this with the participants. This will help the users to know what meetings to attend and come prepared for the sessions.

- To optimize usage of time effectively, schedule main sessions for 90 minutes with 15-minute breaks. Breakout sessions with smaller groups of participants can be 60-minute sessions.

> **Note**
>
> Breakout sessions are useful for teams to discuss in smaller groups and come to a consensus where there is a divergent understanding or misunderstanding of requirements or functionality.

- Assign a junior team member to take care of meeting logistics, such as conference room booking and arranging the resources required during the meeting, including flip charts, markers, sticky notes, a projector, and microphones.

- Identify a scribe for these meetings to take meeting notes and any open questions. This person should be knowledgeable and be able to take notes effectively. Team members when actively discussing or debating will not stop or pause for the note-taker to take notes. The scribe should be able to take notes and elaborate on them in detail and document them for the team. Assigning a junior team member will be very ineffective.

In this section, we learned how prior planning of a few simple but important tasks can help us effectively facilitate our CRPs. Now let us take a look at how these CRP sessions can introduce a few pain points and how we can manage them.

Managing scope creep during CRPs

Planning and conducting many CRPs has its own pros and cons:

- The pros are that we keep everyone informed and on the same page. By collaborating as a group during the CRP session, participants get an opportunity to progressively see the product (functionality) develop. This helps with having open and honest conversations and helps the team steer in the right direction.

- The cons are that there is a lot of room for scope creep. Business stakeholders may realize they failed to identify or inform other business needs. This is a good thing as far as the scope of the CRM phase is concerned, as the main goal here is to identify gaps and improvements.

Let us see the impacts of these pros and cons during each stage of CRPs and how we can manage them to our advantage.

During the scope CRP phase, we certainly should expect many requests, and the majority of them are usually valid. What is in scope and what is not in scope needs to be carefully managed by you as a business analyst and the project manager.

During the design phase, the scope needs to be controlled more aggressively. Anything new cropping up should be evaluated and parked for later release or provided with an alternative simplified solution, and this can be a manual process too. The most important outcome of this design CRP should be identifying usability aspects and non-functional and integration-related requirements.

The build phase should be focused on changes, if any, related to the user interface and user experience. If the design CRP is done productively, we should not see any functional gaps. The tech team may find some non-functional related gaps or technical constraints, and this CRP can help identify them and the technical team can utilize CRM sessions to inform the business stakeholders.

> **Note**
>
> For every constraint that is not feasible, the team needs to come up with a workaround. Without a workaround, the business may not have a way to operate, and you cannot simply say there is a constraint and there is no workaround.

The testing CRP should be more of a demo to all the project team members, and this will help the operations team, training team, and production support teams to understand the functions and features. This will help prepare the team for go-live and post-go-live support.

Any changes—big or small—need to go through the change control team. This team, comprising project sponsors and key project team members, should determine whether this can be absorbed in the release or pushed to the next release. There may be cases where, based on how critical the requirement is, the project date is extended. Make sure the project team documents all additional requests (can be gaps, usability, or enhancement requests) and captures who raised it and when, a brief description, the importance, who it was reviewed by, who accepted it, or if it was kept on hold.

> **Note**
>
> Do not be too rigid in change control. Any low-hanging fruits that are easy to implement should be added to the scope after socializing and agreed on by the team during these CRPs. This is a great motivating factor for CRP participants; you will see better engagement and it will be a win-win scenario for the project team and business team.

> **Note**
>
> The change control team should be participants in these CRP sessions and any new requirements that come up should be added during the breakout session. I would say each day, in the CRP schedule, the change control meeting should take place an hour before the session closes. This session should not take more than 15 to 30 minutes and a decision on go/no-go for additional requirements should be communicated by the close of the session. This saves an enormous amount of time for the whole team.

Reviewing the benefits of CRPs

A well-oiled CRP planned and managed efficiently and effectively will provide many benefits. Let us list some of them here:

- Provides transparency and a common understanding of business needs, the designed solution, the product built, and the final product.

- It is a platform for effective collaboration and idea generation. Effective CRPs facilitated efficiently will let the team interact naturally, allows them to contribute, and creates the most productive outcome.

- Multiple dedicated in-person sessions away from regular work will help create bonds with different team members and enable team members to learn from others. For example, the opportunity/quote management team can learn how the contract team operates and will have an opportunity to understand their business processes and procedures. Similarly, the contract team can learn from the quote team. This helps them empathize with others' work by understanding the intricacies (procedures and policies) and helps bring out the best in people.

- It is an opportunity for stakeholders, SMEs, and project team members to socialize and share experiences. Bonding and creating friendships make future interactions between team members much easier.

- Getting approvals and resolving disagreements will be much faster as all the key team members are in the same sessions. This saves a lot of time for the team members and the project.

- CRPs allow users to see the mockup solution/prototype firsthand. This helps build confidence within not only the participants but also the rest of the team as the session attendees can take the prototype back to their team and communicate to them how their needs are shaping along with the project.

- CRP attendees can help with encouraging and answering queries from their team members. This helps with increased user adoption. Your team can identify a few trailblazers from these sessions and recommend them as SPOCs/champions from their group. These experts can help you bridge the connection between the project and the end user.

- The technical team will benefit immensely as they understand exactly what is needed by the business. Iterative feedback and listening to discussions during CRPs help them deliver a great final product with proposed features and functions.

- The QA (testing) team will benefit by understanding the progression of the needs to the final solution. The testing team will be able to design and test the right test scripts and scenarios and be able to know what to test from a business user perspective. This helps in reducing user acceptance testing defects/queries.

- The training team will be able to prepare and curate the training materials and deliver them productively.

- It is a good place for idea generation. Team members are encouraged to be innovative and free to express their ideas, and this provides your team with an excellent opportunity to capture and document them. Many of them may be off the chart but are excellent ideas that can be implemented in future releases or other projects in your organization.

- It is a good source for project team members to understand the evolution of business needs into a workable solution. This can immensely help the team with the documentation and creation of various project artifacts, such as flow charts, process flows, FDDs, DDDs, and training material.

Practical tips for success

A few practical tips that can be of benefit during your CRP sessions are as follows:

- **Use templates**: Standardize and use the same format for all your CRPs, for example, Agenda, PowerPoint Deck, or an issues/enhancement tracker. This helps participants get comfortable with processes and procedures.

- **Communication with stakeholders and project team members**: Send status reports periodically with action items and due dates to all participants and possibly include their managers and other project team members who are not at the meeting. Make all artifacts available (a read-only version) on a central document management system that team members can access, such as a SharePoint/Teams site or a document management tool of your choice.

- **Engage leads**: Always make it a point to engage leads so that resources assigned to the project are completely motivated for the entire duration of the session. Also, provide feedback, especially where positive, to respective leads. These types of small things make a huge difference to the project.

- **Checkpoints**: Add checkpoints throughout the session, both during and at the end, to get a pulse on how things are progressing. I usually prefer to break the leads and key stakeholders into smaller groups to get a pulse during breaks, and these can be informal check-ins. The whole group can be included in a 15-minute session before ending the session for the day.

- **Lessons learned**: At the end of each session, make it a ritual to note the lessons learned. You'll get valuable insight and feedback that can be incorporated into the next session. Ask each member simple questions, such as the following:

  - What went well?

  - What did not go well? How can it be improved?

  - Any concerns?

  - Suggestions for improvement

- **Next steps**: Just before you end the session, make sure you communicate the next steps with concrete dates, and if possible, include an agenda for the next session.

- **Facilities**: Ensure you have organized the facilities, such as the availability of a meeting room for the entire duration, including all meeting room equipment, such as a projector, whiteboard, flip charts, and telephone system.

- **One note-taker/communicator**: Designate an SME-level person who can understand and take notes. This designated person should be able to distill and refine the notes and prepare minutes for communication to all team members.

- **Centrally located documentation for effective collaboration**: Make sure team members have access to all project-related documents, including any flow charts, process flows, project artifacts, and all meeting minutes. These artifacts should be accessible easily from multiple devices.

- **Give ample time for a Q&A before ending the CRP session**: Stakeholders always love to ask for the next steps and committed dates, so plan and prepare well in advance.

- **Plan to send MoM**: Send meeting minutes on the same day after ending the session to all participants and their leads while the topic is still fresh in their heads.

CRPs are effective methods for team members to experience and see the progression of business needs into a fully functioning business solution. A well-planned and well-spaced CRP during various stages of the project helps identify and resolve issues effectively. These sessions also create opportunities to improve user adoption.

Summary

CRPs help bring the stakeholders, SMEs, architects, and QA, training, and project team members together. Holding these sessions at different stages of the project helps team members collaborate effectively to get a common understanding of business needs and the proposed solution. Well-managed CRPs help teams steer in the right direction, add business value, and avoid any pitfalls along the way, while progressively shaping the final product.

In this chapter, we discussed possible phases where you can plan your prototyping activities. You learned how to effectively facilitate CRP sessions with the right participants and the right timing while keeping an eye on how to manage scope creep. We also saw the benefits of CRP sessions and finally, you learned a few practical tips that possibly benefit and prepare you to be successful at facilitating and managing CRP sessions productively.

In the next chapter, we will cover technical and quality testing approaches and the role of a business analyst in making testing efforts effective and fruitful. We will review how to identify the skills we need our tester to have, help them understand the intricacies of the system and business concepts, and aid them with identifying scenarios and the right set of usable test data.

Questions

1. List a few benefits of CRPs.

2. What is change control and why is it important?

3. Given resource constraints, give one example of how you can optimize a CRP session.

Further reading

-   Conference room pilot: `https://blogs.sap.com/2010/11/14/conference-room-pilot-crp-why-do-you-need-crp-s-for-your-implementation/`

-   Proof of concept: `https://blogs.sap.com/2010/10/27/poc-proof-of-concept/`

9
Technical and Quality Testing

In the previous chapter, we discussed possible phases in which you can effectively plan your prototyping activities. You learned how to effectively facilitate CRP, how to manage scope creep, and some practical tips that will possibly benefit you during your CRP sessions.

Testing is exploring the system's functionality and its usability in a systematic manner to find issues and report them as defects. After getting fixed, these defects will be retested.

In this chapter, we will cover technical and quality testing approaches and the role of the business analyst in making testing efforts effective and fruitful. We will review how to identify the skills needed by our tester, help them understand the intricacies of the system and business concepts, and aid them with identifying scenarios and the right set of usable test data.

We will cover the following topics in this chapter:

- Planning testing activities
- Testing strategy
- Testing approach
- Testing phases
- Types of testing
- Sample test script/case fields
- Benefits of testing
- Practical tips for success

Testing cannot be 100% effective and finding zero defects is not realistic. Start testing as early as possible to uncover any design deficiencies, also called shift-left testing. This will give you room to fix design issues and reduce defects down the line.

Planning testing activities

Software testing should be planned well in advance and the testing team should be involved from the start of the project. On any type of project, we cannot do exhaustive testing and test everything in all possible combinations as it is practically not feasible. Planning helps us make educated choices and make the testing sensible and meaningful. The testing plan is a progressive document and gets refined during the entire course of the project, starting from the requirements phase and getting more granular and refined as we progress.

Let us look at what tests need to be planned during various project phases:

- **User Acceptance Testing (UAT)** planning is done during the requirements specification phase. This test plan outlines what the business users may possibly be testing during the acceptance phase of testing. This UAT plan incrementally gets updated as it helps us with the finalized UAT plan with relevant scope and scenarios.

- **System Integration Testing (SIT)** planning starts during the functional specification phase. SIT involves the overall testing of a software system, including integrations with and to other systems. By the time we have the functional requirements document, we should have a good understanding and scope of system testing and results in the SIT plan.

- The integration testing plan is initiated in the technical specification (HLD) during the architectural design phase. The architect and the technical team will be able to identify and plan for integration testing scenarios to test the integration between various dependent and independent software components.

- The unit testing plan should start as soon as technical development is started and during module/technical development (LLD). This is where the technical team will do detailed testing of each of the units or a combination of a few small units.

> **Note**
> Regression testing, which is rerunning tests to confirm that software features that have already been developed and tested continue to operate as expected when a change is introduced, needs to be planned to include it at every stage of testing. Small modifications can occasionally cause havoc with your implementations when they are implemented without a regression test.

In this chapter, software testing includes hybrid methodology. We combine traditional waterfall development models for certain phases and agile development models or a combination for other phases of the project. *Figure 9.1* is a high-level testing plan sample for a medium- to high-complexity project. This is a simplified sample, and your testing strategy may be more complex and may look very different.

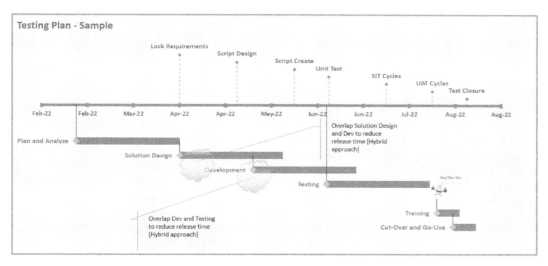

Figure 9.1 – Testing plan

Let's quickly review the stages:

- **Plan and analyze**: By the end of the analysis phases of the project, all the requirements are prioritized, agreed upon, and approved by stakeholders and are baselined for the release. No more changes without CCB approval are entertained, and essentially all requirements for this release are locked. During this phase, we follow the traditional project management methodology.

- **Solution design and development build**: The design and build are staggered and done iteratively using agile methodology to get instant testing feedback. Unit testing and integration testing are part of the build activity and good planning and execution will help us with minimizing defects in the later phases.

- **Testing (system testing and acceptance testing)**: System testing is started after completing unit and integration testing cycles. This is done in traditional waterfall methodology and performed in multiple cycles. Regression testing should be integral to each of the test cycles every time any changes are promoted to avoid breaking any existing critical functionality.

No testing will be planned or performed during the training and go-live phases. These are the last two major project activities, where you start training only after successful test completion and a Go decision is made. After go-live, the technical team will verify code and data migrations, and business analysts, along with key business SMEs, will validate the functionality before opening the system for production usage.

Creating a testing strategy for your project with a timeline and duration will help team members get the complete picture of how, when, and what kind of testing is in scope for the project release.

In the next section, I will walk you through different activities, techniques, and methods associated with a good testing strategy. A good testing strategy needs meticulous planning and keeps testing processes disciplined and predictable.

Testing strategy

A testing strategy helps you define testing levels to be conducted during your project implementation. It provides direction to make sure test objectives are covered and understood by all team members associated with the project. For minor projects, we can collapse testing to fewer levels.

Technical and quality software testing helps us verify and validate that the software product meets the proposed solution with respect to documented and prioritized business requirements:

- **Verify**: Make sure that the output is accurate, true, and justified to ensure the solution follows standards and meets the agreed upon and documented requirements. This verifies we deliver the solution in the right way.

- **Validate**: Check the accuracy of the output, which helps us to ensure the right solutions are implemented that meet the business needs and are usable by the users or the system. This validates that we are implementing the right solution.

Testing levels

Our main goal of testing is to find defects and issues as early in the project as possible. Proper planning and testing ensure that the identified defects are related to specific requirements. Plan to do exhaustive testing as much as possible with available resource constraints and adhere to agreed exit criteria.

For a typical project release, we have four levels of testing, as listed here. For each of the testing levels, we define the testing methods that will be used:

- **Unit testing**: Verify the smallest possible unit (entity) independently for other units (entities). This is done during development to make sure each developed unit works before moving on to the next unit development.

- **Integration testing**: Test plans are developed during the high-level solution design phase to make sure the individual units, when combined, can work together seamlessly. This is done at the module level, or with a few modules grouped together.

- **System testing**: This is done for the entire functionality in scope as well as anything connected to these functions, including integrations. This testing should include functional and non-functional testing.

- **UAT**: This is developed during the requirements phase and should be tested by the end users. The test system should represent a true production system and the business users should test their end-to-end scenarios (a day in the life of a user).

Testing methods

There are two testing methods, which can be used either independently or in combination. These two methods are manual or automated. Based on organizational project requirements, you can use company-approved tools such as HPE Micro Focus and Selenium.

Testing schedule

Based on the complexity of the project, SIT is usually performed in about three cycles, with one regression test as the fourth cycle. For SIT and regression testing, the assumption is that we use a testing tool. Create four folders for each cycle. If not, doing four rounds of testing will take a significant amount of time and we may have to reduce the cycles.

Let's look at a sample testing schedule for a typical global CRM project depicting different cycles of testing done by the QA team and UAT team:

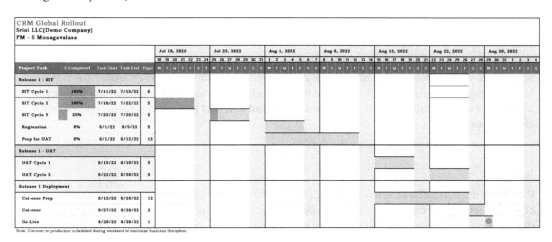

Figure 9.2 – Testing schedule (for a sample CRM global release)

We'll review each cycle in detail:

- **First cycle**: Test a full round of all test cases/scripts. Defects are created for failed test cases and communicated to business analysts to review and send them to the development team for fixing. After these issues are fixed, business analysts will do validation to approve it for retesting in the next cycle. You will find a good number of defects during this cycle. Prepare a summary report for cycle 1.

- **Second cycle**: Review test cases/scripts and adjust them as needed. Rerun failed test cases and make sure the test cases run successfully. Do your second round of testing for all the test cases/scripts and create defects for failed test cases. These defects are reviewed, fixed, validated, and approved for retesting in the next cycle. The defect count should drastically reduce and some enhancement (missed functions or missed scripts) will surface. Prepare a summary report for cycle 2.

- **Third cycle**: Review test cases/scripts and adjust and retest failed cases until they are successfully tested without issues. Do the final round of testing to make sure you have very few or no failed test cases. We should see a handful of failed cases that need to be reviewed and either approved or parked based on business analyst analysis. Prepare a summary report for cycle 3.

- **Regression cycle (cycle 4)**: This cycle will test end-to-end scenario scripts, including integrations with backend systems and any third-party apps of the whole system. This is to ensure we did not accidentally break the existing functionality. Basically, we are testing out functionality the way we do in production. This environment will have a clone of the production data. This means we load any legacy data and use it to test the functionality and integrations. Minimal defects are expected and fixed or parked accordingly. As needed, fixed defects should be retested before approving them for UAT (covered in more detail in *Chapter 11, User Acceptance Testing*).

> **Note**
>
> If you see significant failed test cases during cycle 2, take a pause and review the test cases/scripts and development work. It is worth reviewing as this will cause major issues down the line. If it happens during cycle 3, you need to reconsider revisiting the design and test strategy. Moving forward in this situation will be a disaster and will lead to project remediation efforts after implementation.

> **Note**
>
> If you are migrating large volumes of legacy data from existing legacy systems, you should consider setting up conversion mock cycles. It takes a few cycles to get the data right as it depends on the complexity of your existing metadata. Each cycle helps refine the process, capture the time it takes to perform the tasks, and prepare the deployment team in advance. These data load runs are done after SIT and before regression testing.

Let's take a look at different testing approaches that can help us with testing. Adopt a combination of techniques and methods for each of your testing levels that meets your project needs. Picking the right approach will help you verify and validate that your software functions efficiently.

Testing approach

There are multiple testing approaches that we can utilize during various stages of the project, and they fall under one or more of these techniques/methods/processes:

- **Static testing technique**: Static testing, as the name implies, is a verification process and is done without executing any software functionality. Done by an SME, this technique helps us proactively prevent defects early in the project. Examples are code walk-throughs, technical reviews, inspections, and so on, to project documents such as requirements documents, test scripts, and source code.

- **Dynamic testing technique**: Dynamic testing, as the name suggests, is actual testing conducted on specific functionality and it does the validation of the executed functionality. This is when we uncover many issues. The sooner we unearth them, the better it is for the project. Examples are unit testing, integration testing, system testing, and so on.

- **Passive testing technique**: Passive testing is done from the output of dynamic testing. Team members who are testers will not interact with the functionality in the system but rather analyze the system logs, debug logs, and system traces to look for similar patterns from past projects. This is more like forensic analysis, where samples (that is, logs) are collected and sent to remote labs for analysis.

- **Exploratory testing technique**: Exploratory testing is used on agile projects and testing activities are continuously done iteratively, which encompasses concurrent learning, test designing, test execution, and test result interpretation. This yields excellent testing quality when done by knowledgeable team members. This testing will be helpful when testing completely new functionality for the first time to get rapid feedback.

- **Blackbox testing method**: Blackbox testing aims to test the functionality of the application based on functional specifications with no need to understand how it is implemented internally. This is like when we drive a car – our goal is to go from point A to point B comfortably and safely and we do not need to know how the car engine works or how the A/C unit performs. This testing can be done at any testing level, such as unit, system, integration, and UAT. Business users use this technique while performing acceptance testing.

- **Whitebox testing technique**: Whitebox testing is also called open box testing where users examine the program code logic. This technique helps the technical team look at, improve, and make the code robust and clean. It is helpful when the functionality is complex and technical team members with in-depth knowledge will be able to unearth errors in the hidden code and remove any redundant code. This technique is very useful during unit testing and integration testing.

- **Graybox testing technique**: Graybox testing, as the name suggests, is a mix of the blackbox and whitebox techniques. It is very useful to test functionality related to web-based applications or specific complex domain testing.

There are other approaches that can be used, such as the scenario testing technique, the load testing technique, and so on. Based on the methodology and project implementation cadence of your organization, you can use a combination of these approaches that best fits your project needs. In the next section, we will review different testing phases of our testing life cycle.

Testing phases

Software testing, for the most part, follows the following six phases. Based on your project, you can merge or skip some phases. Before testing can be started, we need to establish test entry/exit criteria. These testing phases are important to SIT and are performed by an independent testing team, also called the **QA** team.

Let's list the entry/exit criteria for typical software testing:

- Requirements are prioritized and finalized
- Acceptance criteria for testing have been agreed
- Testing phases and methods are established

Let's quickly review each of these phases:

- **Requirements analysis**: During this phase, testing team members understand the requirements in detail from a testing perspective, so that they can plan and estimate the testing scope and efforts.

- **Planning**: During this phase, the QA test lead determines the test strategy for various types of testing, testing effort and other estimates, testing tools, resource planning, and so on for the project.

- **Test case/script design and development**: The testing team identifies and prepares scripts/scenarios and each requirement is mapped to one or more of the test cases/scripts. Test data requirements are identified, created, and reviewed for tester usage.

- **Environment setup**: During this phase, the proper testing environment is identified and set up. Setting up includes moving all the configuration metadata and actual test data along with access to user records. This phase also makes sure the environment is ready for use and is stable by doing a smoke test.

- **Execution**: During this phase, the actual execution of test cases based on the test plan is performed by the testers. The tester will execute test scripts and report issues by creating defects. During this phase, all fixed defects will be retested in all test cases, executed with a status of pass or fail. Also, every test case is mapped to requirements and a **requirements traceability matrix (RTM)** is created to ensure that every test case can be traced to requirements and marked with an execution status.

- **Closure**: During this phase, test coverage reports, defect reports, issue dashboards, and test closure reports are generated. After SIT, the testing team will perform smoke and sanity tests in a production environment to make sure the system is ready and stable for UAT.

Note the following:

- Smoke testing (system stability) is a software testing method to confirm that the build solution is stable, important features work as expected, and there are no showstoppers in the build that is under testing.

- Sanity testing (system rationality) is a quick and basic test to determine whether a particular software functionality is behaving correctly at a basic level before subjecting it to the next stage of rigorous testing.

In the next section, we will learn about different types of testing that are available for us to perform testing on functional and non-functional aspects of our software functionality.

Types of testing

Let us review some important testing types in the context of SaaS CRM implementations.

We will focus on testing related to SaaS model software. With SaaS providers such as Salesforce, HubSpot, or NetSuite, we do not need to worry much about performance, scalability, and security issues if we follow the software provider's guidelines and best practices.

There are two main types of testing that we are interested in in this chapter:

- **Functional testing**: This is a software testing technique to test the features and functionality of the developed solution. Functional testing includes positive, negative, and boundary scenarios. Let us look at some common functional testing techniques:

  - **Unit testing** (also called development unit testing): Unit testing is done by the technical team member on individual units/modules to determine whether there are any bugs in the code. Following the unit test life cycle, a unit test helps with identifying issues early and enables us to reduce the cost of testing.

  - **Integration testing**: This involves individual units being combined and tested to ensure individual modules work together seamlessly without any issues as one single entity.

  - **System testing**: All components of the system are tested to evaluate system compliance against specified business/functional requirements.

  - **Interface testing**: System components are tested to confirm data and controls are exchanged as planned. In the event of failure to exchange, exceptions are handled accordingly.

  - **Regression**: This involves re-executing a specific set of test cases that may be impacted due to code changes. This is to confirm the stability of the product due to changing requirements. The main aim of regression testing is to uncover issues in previously working software that have been introduced unintentionally because of the change.

- **UAT**: This is testing performed to confirm the correctness and completeness of the business requirements specification. This is the final stage of testing before the specification can be promoted to production.

- **Non-functional testing**: This is a software testing technique that examines a system's non-functional attributes such as performance, usability, reliability, scalability, security, and so on. It is designed to test the preparedness and readiness of a system. Let's look at a few techniques:

  - **Documentation testing**: This involves testing documented artifacts such as the functional requirements document, test plan, test cases, and static code analysis. Salesforce provides the Apex testing framework for Apex test classes to define and generate code coverage. This is to ensure correctness, completeness, and clarity.

  - **Installation testing**: This testing is to make sure the installed components or software are working as expected. For example, installing a plugin such as the D&B Hoovers managed AppExchange package in Salesforce.

  - **Performance testing**: This is performed to confirm system responsiveness, availability, reliability, stability, scalability, and so on, and to measure the following quality attributes of the system:

    - Load testing

    - Stress testing

    - Endurance (or soak) testing

    - Spike testing

  - **Security testing**: This testing is used to determine that the system protects data, authorizes and authenticates the right users, and renders intended functionality.

During SIT and UAT phases of testing, the majority of these functional and non-functional test scripts are executed as per the test plan. Issues identified during testing are reported as defects and retested after the defects are addressed by your development team.

Defects identified during testing will impact test execution. Test defects are classified as critical, high, medium, and low. A critical defect can require a simple fix but if it impacts multiple test scripts, it is the one with the highest priority for our testing. A medium defect can involve complex changes but may impact only one or two test cases and so it can wait until others are fixed. This severity value gives us insight into which defects need to be prioritized.

> **Note**
> Test severity is not the same as business priority. When we say the test severity is critical, that means the tester cannot move forward with testing for that module unless this defect is addressed.

Let us look at a sample test script/test case template. These are typical fields that we would see while creating a test scenario. This can be used for manual testing or can be used to upload our business specification into a testing tool.

Sample test script/case fields

Test scenarios are high-level actions that provide an overview of what needs to be tested. They help in the testing of end-to-end functionality. Test cases are low-level activities and help with thorough testing of the application. They enable us to test small parts of functionality in detail. Each test script can have multiple test cases.

The following are some of the important fields that can be used to create test scripts/cases:

- Test Script ID: TS-Account Management-001

- Test Script Name: The user will be able to create and edit accounts in Salesforce

- Test Script Description: The user will be able to create and edit account records in Salesforce after entering the required fields and will be able to save successfully

- Pre-conditions: The user will have appropriate access and be able to log into the Salesforce system via a browser and/or mobile apps

- Test System Name: SIT

- BRD ID: BRD-R1-1.001

- Complexity: Medium

- Variations: 6 (Sales Analyst, Sales Manager, Service Analyst, Service Manager, Planning, and Legal)

- Database Table/Object name: Account

- Test Case ID: TC-Account Management-001-Create-01

- Cycle: 1

- Planned Execution Date: MM/DD/YYYY

- Test Case Description: The user will be able to create a prospect and be able to input all required and optional fields and be able to save the record

- Variation Description: The user (sales analyst) will not be able to delete the prospect record

- Test Case Result: Output from the testing (example – user able to successfully create a prospect)

- Responsible Tester: XXXXXXXX

- Evidence: Links to screenshots.

- Results: Final result, which can be Pass/Fail/Not in scope

Creating test scripts/cases simplifies your review and approval process as Excel documents can be shared via a central shared site. After approval, they can be loaded onto a testing tool of your choice.

Figure 9.3 shows a sample SIT test script:

Figure 9.3 – SIT test script

Sample templates can be utilized for UAT too. Feel free to add/remove fields as fits your project testing.

Benefits of testing

Proper software testing, when planned and executed well, will yield many benefits. Project success or failure and user adoption greatly depend on how well the system responds and makes sure that the end users do not run into post-production deployment issues.

Some of the benefits that can be realized are the following:

- The risk of failure of the product after deployment into production can be greatly minimized.

- Integrations with other systems work seamlessly, and in the case of failure due to any reason, there is a restart mechanism or a documented way to handle the issue.

- By delivering quality software products, end users do not face issues and are able to perform their business without needing to worry about software issues.

- An issue-free software functionality or system will build trust and drive business user adoption. We will have satisfied business users/customers.

- It's a great opportunity to verify and validate the security features of the software functionality and provide software free from any vulnerabilities. Vulnerabilities in test systems can be controlled and fixed with minimal risk. The same thing happening with end users in production systems can be a major risk.

- Finally, good testing results in cost-effectiveness. Spending a little bit more during testing pays off manyfold in the long run, in addition to many other benefits.

Practical tips for success

A few practical tips that can benefit you during your testing activities are the following:

- Do not skip the test strategy. Make a checklist for the test strategy.

- Where possible, use automated tools, especially for SIT and regression tests. Regression tests must be run multiple times whenever an issue is fixed.

- UAT should be done by business users who are SMEs in their area. Following prior documented test scripts is very ineffective. In addition to test scripts, business users should run through ad hoc real-life scenarios. If there are any issues, this is our last opportunity to find and fix them.

- The QA team or SIT team should be made up of independent team members with good system knowledge with some level of business domain knowledge. The technical team members who developed the application should be the last people to do SIT.

- Team members should take static testing seriously. A review of the static artifacts by SMEs and leads helps clarify and keep the documents clean and unambiguous. The identification of issues with static testing does not require code fixing and retesting. All that is needed are a few hours of dedicated time from experts.

- Perform code reviews and functionality demos within the project team, and especially the technical team, where the leads and experts can provide immediate feedback.

- The project's test lead and business analyst should spend time triaging defects. Try to group similar defects by what is called defect clustering. We often find 70%-80% of defects from 20-30% of the functionality.

- At the end of each cycle, revise and update test cases. Periodic reviews keep the test cases current and relevant.

- Software applications are accessed by users on various devices and browsers. Make sure to do regression tests on all browsers and devices.

- It is okay if a few defects cannot be resolved, and I have never seen a defect-free implementation. If the defect is not business-critical, or if it is critical but there is a workaround agreed by business stakeholders, then this defect can be parked for future release prioritization.

- Create and test reports and dashboards. This test system should have a good set of data for SIT and should mirror the production instance for UAT.

- Always include sufficient test cases to test functionality with loaded legacy data. The data converted from a legacy system should work as well as new records created in the system.

- Facilitate and capture feedback from team members, especially around testing activities. These lessons learned from documents will be valuable artifacts for your future releases.

- Do not forget to acknowledge and recognize individuals and teams who went above and beyond and helped with testing activities.

That brings us to the end of this chapter.

Summary

Software testing is an extremely important activity on any project. Testing is not just a phase that can be done at the end of development, but rather a continuous process that requires the QA/testing team's involvement in all phases of the project. The testing process starts with team members understanding the business requirements and being able to plan and come up with a solid test strategy. The testing team should be able to understand the scope, tools, and methods they can use to make the testing process effective and productive.

In this chapter, we discussed the importance of a good testing strategy and how it can benefit our project team with testing activities. You learned about various testing approaches, phases, and types. Finally, we concluded the chapter with how and why testing can benefit your projects and some good practical tips from my experience. These practical tips will help you avoid a lot of pain points and save you time during your test cycles.

In the next chapter, we will cover dependencies between test cases and requirements, and how to trace them and establish 100% test case coverage. You will learn the importance of the RTM and what to capture in the matrix. We will also discuss the advantages of good requirements traceability and a sample RTM template.

Questions

1.   List some testing tools that help with automated testing.

2.   Is regression testing the same as retesting?

3.   Think of a few examples of blackbox testing.

Further reading

- *Secrets to Successful Data Conversions* (https://sapinsider.org/secrets-to-successful-data-conversions/)

- *The different types of testing in software* (https://www.atlassian.com/continuous-delivery/software-testing/types-of-software-testing)

- https://en.wikipedia.org/wiki/Software_testing

10
Requirements Traceability Matrix

In the previous chapter, we discussed the importance of a good testing strategy and how it can help us to identify issues early in the project so that we can deliver usable functionality that meets our stakeholder needs, and at the same time, reduce costs by addressing issues as soon as possible.

In this chapter, we will understand the importance of the relationship between requirements and various project artifacts and how they help us establish traceability. Requirements traceability guides us to ensure the projects proceed on the right track and address issues along the way. It helps us in identifying and bridging gaps to make sure each of the business requirements provides the intended functionality and fulfills business needs. We will see how to link requirements to project deliverables and make sure we have 100% coverage. We will also see how to identify inconsistencies with testing artifacts and overall testing execution status and hence the progress of the project.

We will cover the following topics:

- Understanding the importance of a **Requirements Traceability Matrix (RTM)**
- Learning what to capture in an RTM
- Exploring types of traceability
- Reviewing an RTM template sample
- Benefits of an RTM
- Practical tips for success

An RTM is a worksheet that consists of all your prioritized requirements for the project release and corresponding test scripts and test cases with the status in addition to a reference to other project artifacts. This helps the project team to understand the level of testing activities performed or yet to be performed for each functionality and ensure that no requirement is left uncovered.

Let's look at the importance of the RTM in the next section.

Understanding the importance of an RTM

Most often, an RTM is created during the test planning phase of the project. It will be very useful and handy if you start preparing this document right from the requirement phase and keep adding details as you progress through each phase of the project. This will make it easier to capture details accurately without missing out on any important items. Collaborating and reviewing this document along with other artifacts during each stage of the project enables us to maintain an active and up-to-date version of the requirements traceability.

Think of requirements traceability as the way we track the progress of the movement of goods from one point to another. Let's assume a customer purchased a car. If there is a problem with some part, the car company can trace back and check where the part originated from. Similarly, if there is a defect identified with a specific part (say, a seat belt), the company can identify the customers and send a recall notice (to fix or replace the seat belt at their nearest dealer) to them. Requirements traceability does the same thing for software requirements. Any defects along the way can be traced bi-directionally and addressed efficiently so that they are accurately solved and business user requirements are delivered as originally proposed.

Issues are unavoidable, no matter what they might be. How soon we identify them and how fast we address them makes all the difference. Identifying and fixing issues or bugs needs to be made as seamless as possible for the end users. The majority of the time, users should not even realize that these issues existed. A good example is regular updates to your laptop's software and patches. These are fixes for bugs or improvements and the majority of the users do not even realize or experience the issues before they are patched.

I have listed here some of the reasons for having a well-documented requirements traceability matrix. This document is more valuable if your projects are relatively complex to highly complex. It does not take much time to create an RTM but the value it adds can be in many folds. Let us look at a few of them. A requirements traceability matrix aids the projects team in the following ways:

- Helping us ensure that each of the prioritized BRD requirements is tested adequately and there is complete coverage

- Establishing transparency of processes and the ability to track changes

- Ensuring that the delivered solution fulfills all requirements and helping prevent failures by identifying gaps

- Finding defects, issues, and enhancements during project implementation at every stage of the project and helping us quickly identify the root cause and thus save time

- Providing context to the development team so that they can refer to the business requirement or trace forward to test coverage

- Streamlining the development life cycle by connecting project artifacts

- Defining expectations for the testing team

- Ensuring the right product is built the right way

Here we looked at a few good reasons for the use of an RTM. In the next section, let us see what elements to capture in the RTM and make it useful and helpful to understand and, at the same time, get a complete view at a glance.

Learning what to capture in an RTM

A well-designed RTM should have enough fields for project team members to get a 360-degree view of the linkage from the business requirement to the test case status. Too many fields lead to confusion, and too few fields make it incomplete. I captured a few important fields here for reference so that users at a first glance will be able to trace the artifact bi-directionally. You can add more fields if it makes sense for your project implementation, and you can always hide a few fields and unhide them when needed.

We can utilize prior artifacts such as business requirements documents, functional documents, solution design documents, wireframes, process flows, test scripts, and test cases, and link key fields to establish and capture traceability. We can either create a long document with all possible fields from these artifacts or a simplified version with a few key unique fields. Based on these key unique fields, you can refer to respective documents to get granular details to understand the cause of test failure or scope creep.

The following are the fields that I prefer to report in the RTM, and it is your choice to pick your own set of fields as long as you can establish effective traceability:

- BRD requirement ID: Requirement ID from our business requirement document

- BRD requirement description

- Conceptual diagram name

- Process flow name

- FDD ID: Functional requirement ID

- Solution design document name

- Functional area: For example, account management, opportunity management, and so on

- DDD name: Design document ID

- Test script ID: Script ID

- Test case ID: Case ID

- Test script variants: For example, sales analysts from different business units may see a different field and picklist values

- User type: Role of the user being tested. For example, sales agent, sales manager, sales operations, marketing user, and so on

- Test case description: Brief description of what is tested
- Status: Pass, fail, or invalid

Now we have defined a list of RTM fields, but before we can capture details under these fields, let us see the types of traceability and how this set of fields helps us with different traceability types.

Exploring types of traceability

There are three types of traceability. We move from left to right, right to left, or either way. They are as follows:

- **Forward traceability**: We start with a prioritized requirement and trace it each way to see the design, development, and testing progress in the right direction toward our proposed and intended functionality. Essentially, it helps us to make sure that we captured the requirement correctly, we have all the information related to the requirement, and that this is the right requirement.

- **Backward traceability**: We start tracing backward from specific phases of projects. It can be from test script to development to design to the business requirement, or it can be from solution design to functional design to business requirement. This is to make sure we are doing the right thing and staying on the right track and not going off course. This type of traceability ensures that we should be able to trace each individual functionality developed in the system back to the prioritized business requirement. Essentially, it helps us to make sure we deliver the right solution, that the requirement is valid, and that the solution adds business value.

- **Bi-directional traceability**: Both ways, depending on the given scenario. If we see a failed test case, we can trace it back and get to the root cause. If we had additional requirements, such as scope changes, we could help with analyzing the impacts of changes to requirements.

In addition to tracing business requirements to the end solution and vice versa, we need to consider mapping them to the following entities to make it complete:

- **Business units**: This helps us ensure that we do not miss any operational steps performed by specific business roles (sales analyst, service analyst, planning, and so on) and aligns with the business process flow steps. Any missed and redundant activities or tasks can be identified and fixed.

- **User role**: This helps us identify and fix all steps the user performs while using the system. For example, the service analyst's role is to create and manage cases and this may be their primary function, whereas the sales analyst's role is to capture and qualify leads and close more deals.

- **Database object**: Tracing to and from DB objects helps us with security requirements in confirming availability. For example, service agents do not need access to campaign management. Another example is CRUD permission to the object to determine who can and cannot create, read, update, and delete the record.

We have learned about the types of traceability and three distinct mapping entities. Now, let's look at a sample RTM template and see for ourselves how it can help us see the traceability and various data points and artifacts in the traced path.

Reviewing an RTM template sample

Let us look at sample RTM matrix data. You can use various RTM tools available in the market based on the nature and complexity of your project release. In our case, I am using a simple Excel spreadsheet, as shown here. This matrix is a simplified version of a more complex RTM. An RTM for a complex project will span multiple columns and rows and does not fit here as a screenshot. You can add more columns and capture details related to BRD, FDD, and so on, and keep the columns hidden. When you see a failed test case, you can unhide the columns to get details from one single document.

Requirements Traceability Matrix													
BRD Requirement Id	BRD Requirement Description	Conceptual Diagram Name	Process Flow Name	Solution Design Document Name	Functional Area	FDD Id	DDD Name	Test Script Id	Test Case Id	Test Script Variants	User Type	Test Case Description	Status
RQ_ID001	Account Management	None	Account Flow	Release1_Track01	Accounts	FDD_001	DDD_001	Script-101	TST_001/TST_002	2	3	TC Description_001	Pass
						FDD_002	DDD_002	Script-102	TST_003/TST_005	2	3	TC Description_002	Pass
						FDD_003	DDD_003	Script-103	TST_006/TST_008	1	3	TC Description_003	Pass
RQ_ID002	Contact management	None	None	Release1_Track01	Contacts	FDD_004	DDD_004	Script-104	TST_00x/TST_00y	2	2	TC Description_004	Pass
						FDD_005	DDD_005	Script-105	TST_00x/TST_00y	3	2	TC Description_005	Fail
						FDD_006	DDD_006	Script-106	TST_00x/TST_00y	1	2	TC Description_006	Pass
RQ_ID003	Case management	None	Case Flow	Release1_Track01	Cases	FDD_007	DDD_007	Script-107	TST_00x/TST_00y	5	3	TC Description_007	Fail
						FDD_008	DDD_008	Script-108	TST_00x/TST_00y	4	3	TC Description_008	Pass
RQ_ID004	Opportunity Management	Opportunity diagram	Opportunity Flow	Release1_Track02	Opportunities	FDD_009	DDD_009	Script-109	TST_00x/TST_00y	2	3	TC Description_009	Pass
						FDD_010	DDD_010	Script-110	TST_00x/TST_00y	2	3	TC Description_010	Pass
						FDD_011	DDD_011	Script-111	TST_00x/TST_00y	2	3	TC Description_011	Pass
RQ_ID005	Quote Management	None	Quote/Quote Approval flow	Release1_Track02	Quotes	FDD_012	DDD_012	Script-112	TST_00x/TST_00y	3	1	TC Description_012	Pass
						FDD_013	DDD_013	Script-113	TST_00x/TST_00y	3	1	TC Description_013	Pass
RQ_ID006	Quote Approval Rule Matrix	None	Quote/Quote Approval flow	Release1_Track02	Quotes	FDD_014	DDD_014	Script-114	TST_00x/TST_00y	2	2	TC Description_014	Pass
						FDD_015	DDD_015	Script-115	TST_00x/TST_00y	1	2	TC Description_015	Pass
						FDD_016	DDD_016	Script-116	TST_00x/TST_00y	1	1	TC Description_016	Pass
RQ_ID007	Product Alignment	Product Alignment diagram	None	Release1_Track03	Products	FDD_017	DDD_017	Script-117	TST_00x/TST_00y	3	2	TC Description_017	In Progress
						FDD_018	DDD_018	Script-118	TST_00x/TST_00y	3	2	TC Description_018	No Run
RQ_ID008	Campaign Management	None	None	Release1_Track03	Campaign	FDD_019	DDD_019	Script-119	TST_00x/TST_00y	5	3	TC Description_019	No Run

Figure 10.1 – Requirements Traceability Matrix

Based on this data and using test case artifacts, we can create a sample traceability chart, as shown next. There are many tools available that can help you with creating complex and more sophisticated traceability matrices:

Requirements Traceability Chart													
Test Script Coverage				Test Coverage		Business Requirement ID							
Test Script ID	Complexity	Variants	User Types	Required	Actual	RQ_ID001	RQ_ID002	RQ_ID003	RQ_ID004	RQ_ID005	RQ_ID006	RQ_ID007	RQ_ID008
Script-101	H	5	3	15	15								
Script-102	H	6	2	12	10								
Script-103	M	9	3	27	21								
Script-104	M	6	3	18	18								
Script-105	H	6	1	6	6								
Script-106	L	4	3	12	12								
Script-107	M	6	2	12	12								

Figure 10.2 – Requirements Traceability Chart

Let's review each script. There are three good scenarios here. Let us take a look at each one of them in detail:

- **Scenario 1: Script-101** is a highly complex script with five variants and three user types. So, the test coverage required to be covered at a minimum will be 5x3=15. We can have more, but at a minimum, we need to test 15 scripts. In reality, our tester tested all 15 and this fulfills business requirements **RQ_ID001** and **RQ_ID002**. This is what we want, and all is good so far. This is the same with **Script-106** and **Script-107**.

- **Scenario 2**: In coverage of **Script-102** and **Script-103**, we have a gap in required versus actual. In the matrix, we do not see any testing done for **RQ_ID005** and **RQ_ID006**. So, from this simplified matrix, we are able to quickly identify that the testing either failed or was not yet executed for these two scripts. Based on the test script ID and business requirement ID, we can refer to the requirement traceability matrix and identify the corresponding project artifacts such as FDD, DDD, and process flows, which can tremendously help the project team to quickly find the source so that further analysis can be done to address the failed test script.

- **Scenario3**: For **Script-105**, we see that all six test scripts were executed and none of them are aligned or belong to any of our test scripts. There are a few options here: test scripts may be redundant, may be missed on being assigned to prioritized requirements, or we may have tested requirements not in scope for our release. From this simple chart, you can identify them quickly and fix the chart by either removing the test scripts from our testing scope or tagging the correct business requirement in the RTM.

I can go on with many examples, but these three scenarios should have provided you with a good idea of how you can trace with an RTM in either direction.

Now, let's see a few benefits of an RTM in the next section.

Benefits of an RTM

Some of the benefits of an effective, well-designed, and well-managed traceability matrix include helping us identify missed test coverage and hence potential issues that can be addressed prior to releasing the solution to the end user. Here's a detailed list:

- Traceability to the best possible extent to ensure all important requirements are not missed after production deployment.

- Traceability helps the team with auditing from requirements to the final solution and ensures transparency.

- An RTM is a very helpful artifact to meet compliance needs, especially with financial, healthcare, and other industries.

- Establishes trust with stakeholders, SMEs, and other team members as we will be able to prove our traceability, that the project work progressed as planned, and correct products were delivered.

- In case of change requests that crop up during various phases in projects, this helps the project team and CAB approvers evaluate the impact of potential changes and helps with related impact analysis.

- Scope changes can be easily managed as any deviations in scope can be traced to missing design elements and test scripts.

- One very important benefit that I found extremely helpful is that it allows us to identify dependencies between requirements. We can uncover missing dependencies.

- It saves time and adds efficiency as any team member will be able to identify and trace back from failed test cases to requirements and vice versa.

- It helps with better collaboration and transparency. Anyone on the project can know exactly the status of the testing scripts.

Given that there are so many benefits that can be achieved with requirements traceability, it is worth putting effort into an RTM.

Practical tips for success

Listed here are a few practical tips that added value to my own RTMs:

- RTMs can get very complex. No matter what tool you use, try to keep it simple and extract an Excel or PDF version (at least one daily snapshot) and make it available to all project team members.

- Certain business rules cannot be traced, and you do not waste project time and effort writing test scripts for those unless they are critical for your organization. For example, a user will use only company domain-specific emails and not personal emails, or users should be on the company network/VPN to access an application.

- Keep your RTM current. Anytime there are changes to any project artifacts such as BRD, FDD, DDD, and test scripts, make sure the RTM is reviewed and updated.

- The RTM responsibility should be given to only a few team members so that only they are authorized to make additions or updates to the matrix. Always keep track of the version, even if you manage the RTM on a simple Excel sheet.

- Traceability should be reviewed, verified, validated, and agreed on by key project team members. This is especially critical for non-functional system architectural requirements that improve the quality and usability of the system.

- Business analysts facilitating a 1- to 2-hour session and walkthrough of the RTM with a technical team and testing team will aid everyone with effective knowledge transition compared to just sharing the documents.

That brings us to the end of this chapter.

Summary

In this chapter, we discussed various aspects of traceability and how it can help the team identify and fix variances between the actual business requirements and the final functional solution. We got a chance to discuss the importance of good requirements traceability matrix, different types of traceability, advantages, and a sample scenario. We concluded the chapter with RTM benefits that you may be able to realize in your projects, and some good practical tips, which will help guide you to create a productive RTM.

In the next chapter, we will explore why user acceptance is crucial for a successful go-live and how we can improve user adoption and gain trust by working with business stakeholders and helping them test real-life business end-to-end scenarios. We will explore how to focus on getting feedback on usability when the user does end-to-end scenario testing.

Questions

1.   How does forward traceability help us?

2.   What does backward traceability do?

3.   Forward traceability is a verification process. True or false?

4.   Backward traceability is a validation process. True or false?

Further reading

- The links in *Chapter 29, Software Requirements*, of *Software Requirements 3, 3e (Developer Best Practices)*, by Karl Wiegers and Joy Beatty, Microsoft Press US

Part 3:
End User Testing, Communication, Training, and Support

In this last part, you will learn the final phases of project activities that are centered around end users' involvement with user acceptance testing, well-curated communication, and impactful and tailored training. You will also learn how to plan and execute production support activities so that users can use the newly implemented system functionality effectively and efficiently. We will explore various methods, tools, techniques, and real-life scenarios that you can use during your project phases, which will help you deliver exceptional system usability and user adoption.

This is where the rubber meets the road, and we are at the most critical phase where all the hard work pays off. If correctly managed, you will be in a better position to address these challenges.

We will address some of the key challenges faced during this phase:

- Insufficient testing by a few random available team members testing Salesforce applications rather than involving advocates and champions from diverse groups who can do complete end-to-end scenario testing

- End users do not know how to use the Salesforce system - providing a one-time training for such large group and not identifying this as a learning process for them

- Unplanned or under-planned support model resulting in frustrated end users, which in turn affects system usage and adoption

- Not keeping users engaged after project completion by way of user forums, feedback sessions, and so on

The following chapters will be covered under this part:

- *Chapter 11, User Acceptance Testing*
- *Chapter 12, Communication and Knowledge Management*
- *Chapter 13, End User Training*
- *Chapter 14, Post-Go-Live Support / User Forums*

11
User Acceptance Testing

In the previous chapter, we discussed various aspects of traceability and how it can help the team identify and fix variance between the actual business requirements and the final functional solution. We had the chance to discuss which key elements to capture, the types of requirements for a good traceability matrix, and the advantages we can derive from being able to trace requirements effectively and address any gaps in coverage.

In this chapter, we will explore why user acceptance is crucial for a successful go-live. We will look at how we can improve user adoption and gain trust by working with business testers. We will see how we can work with business users and help them test real-life business end-to-end scenarios. We will explore and see the ways to focus on getting feedback on usability by encouraging testers to follow through with end-to-end scenarios and exploratory testing.

The primary goal of **user acceptance testing** (**UAT**) is to ensure that the new functionality does exactly what it intended to do and meets the business requirements. UAT is a formal type of testing; it needs to be planned and executed in a structured way and provide objective evidence that the system is performing as intended and in line with the agreed acceptance criteria. UAT needs to include scenarios that involve end-to-end testing and cover all business processes that are directly and indirectly impacted by these changes.

In this chapter, we will discuss the following topics around UAT:

- Identifying the right set of UAT users
- Learning how to help UAT users test effectively
- Getting feedback on usability
- Exploring the need for UAT
- Reviewing the benefits of UAT
- Practical tips for success

Identifying the right set of UAT users

Finding and staffing the right testing team member with the right skills, business knowledge, and right attitude plays a very important role during UAT. For UAT to be effective, there are multiple dimensions. The most important dimension in testing is the tester who is performing UAT.

UAT testers should be involved right from the start of the projects and they usually are your key stakeholders who help define, refine, prioritize, and approve your project requirements. These users are involved in every phase and are intimately aware of various project artifacts at every stage of the project. They should be aware of how things have taken shape along the course of the project phases. They are the recipients of the final software solution and they have the commitment and attitude to make the project successful. UAT gives these experts an opportunity to test-drive production in terms of working systems and helps us identify potential real issues related to functionality, usability, and accessibility. Your team needs to make every effort to identify this one critical and very important dimension – the UAT tester. This identified UAT tester with a good understanding helps achieve the desired results of the project. You can guide the tester with the following dimensions to make their work effective:

- **Testing coverage**: The tester should understand the scope of testing and what gets tested. This means they need to understand and be able to navigate the software system and related tools.

- **Reason for testing**: The tester should understand why they are testing. This means they need to have in-depth knowledge of the business and be able to think and do the testing creatively and effectively and understand the risk and problems that can be mitigated by effective testing.

- **Understand testing methods and tools**: They can use a combination of various methods such as black-box, exploratory, and others depending on what the situation demands. They should use their creativity and be innovative with testing.

- **Evaluation**: To be able to evaluate the end results of testing, they should understand the business requirements and the business priorities. They should be part of the project from the start and involved in defining the acceptance criteria, and be able to confirm what a passing or failed test case means.

> **Note**
>
> Do not choose somebody or anybody who is free and available from the business side as a tester just for the sake of doing UAT. You would be better off skipping UAT altogether if this were the case. Another alternative, as the last resort, is that the business analyst and a few project SMEs can perform UAT, although it may not be as effective as testing on the part of the actual business users. The very purpose of UAT is for your end user to verify and confirm that the solution meets their business needs. If users do not do UAT, you will miss the opportunity to identify issues and get feedback early on. This leads to a cascading effect, and eventually, you run into the risk of poor user adoption.

You should have a diverse group of experts identified as testers from your business verticals. These testers should understand their businesses and how various business functions interact within and outside their business units. They should also understand and be conversant with the software systems and tools. It may so happen that it's your first project release: in this case, identify and train the right individuals who are committed to being the testers on subsequent releases along your roadmap. Retaining the majority of the same business testers helps speed up the testing process.

Typical UAT testers are key stakeholders from each of the functional areas – planning or sales operations teams, business analysts (more for informal testing, reproducing errors to identify defects, and retesting test scenarios to fix defects), and training team members.

> **Note**
>
> You may be surprised that you need business analysts and training team members to be involved in UAT. I strongly encourage you as a business analyst to do so. Just try one time and you will see the following benefits:
>
> - Business analysts can do testing quickly and identify and fix issues, plus by running the test scripts, they can help fix ambiguous ones. This also helps you to aid business users during their testing and be able to understand issues and collaborate effectively.
>
> - Training team members will be able to understand the complete process and experience how the users use the system. This helps trainers in preparing or reviewing and fine-tuning training artifacts, as well as during training end users.

Learning how to help UAT users test effectively

User acceptance testers are like expert samplers. If you can get the right expert with excellent knowledge of the business domain and (to some extent) the software system that will help the project team, you will get the right feedback. It's up to the UAT test lead to provide them with the right tools and techniques and define the appropriate scope of testing so that they can complete UAT within the given time and resource constraints. We need to provide the right tools at the right time so that the business tester can do what they are good at and is tasked with doing.

Let us look at some key success factors that help us get testing done effectively:

- **Get the right UAT testers**: Get a diverse group of individuals who are super users, SMEs, business champions, planning team members, and sales operators. Their time, expertise, and business needs are the drivers for successful testing.

- **Involvement from the requirements phase**: The identification of these individuals (at least some of them) should be planned and involved right from the requirements prioritization stage. This helps them understand project priorities and set expectations about why some requirements are in scope and why others are not. They also get involved in understanding the current and proposed business process flows.

- **Walkthrough/training**: Before we start UAT, these sets of users need to be trained on how to use the system. Plan to walk them through the entire system end to end, even if they may not be testing the entire functionality. This helps them understand how different features are linked and dependent.

- **Help them with navigation**: Provide them with a crash course including how to log into the system and reset their password. This should include screen features, data views, reports, collaboration features, and print screen features. Make sure to review third-party apps and any integration with pertinent systems. Provide a one-page cheat sheet outlining the most commonly used functions and navigation items.

- **Recurring daily checkpoints**: I always prefer to facilitate two meetings to go through any issues, concerns, and queries. It's always good to share a screen online or through a projector to allow the tester to articulate their concerns or findings better. This also helps other testers see how a specific business user approached testing and their thought process while doing so.

- **Access to systems**: Make sure your tester has access to all the relevant systems that they are supposed to test. For example, say that they are testing functionality account management in Salesforce and account management utilizes a third-party app such as D&B Hoovers, a KYC system, and an MDM system. Similarly, quote management may be integrated into CPQ. Access to this system should be made as seamless as possible; if not, a 4-hour test will take days, plus a lot of frustration. Also, make sure users are provided appropriate access reflecting the security model and not system admin-level access during UAT.

- **Teaching skills needed for testing**: Help testing with other tools such as the testing tool, where they may be running the scripts, screenshot tools, and recording tools to capture test evidence that may be needed for later auditing. If they must test on mobile devices, such as an iPad or Chromebook, make sure that you get a few loaners from your IT department and that all apps are made available for testing on these devices.

- **Provide test data**: Providing enough test data for testing in addition to creating data will be very vital for effective testing. Users should be able to use existing data to make updates and see that the existing data is usable and works with integration, just like new records created by users. This should be in line with production data quality with scrambled fields wherever you have sensitive MNPI data. A good volume of test data will help with test reports and dashboards too.

- **Exit criteria**: Help the testers understand when they should mark a test case as passing or failed. The exit criteria should be explained and agreed upon with testers before commencing with UAT. If certain functionality fails even though it meets the exit criteria, but the business SME thinks otherwise, then the exit criteria need to be fixed. They need to understand the rules of testing and they cannot make up rules while testing.

- **Project team hotline**: During the duration of testing, make sure someone from the project team is available to answer the UAT testers' queries. These could be functionality-related, test script-related, access-related, or anything else related to testing.

> **Note**
>
> We can never reach a zero-issue stage. So, define what it means when we say testing is completed. The key term we need to define during the project planning phase is to define and understand the acceptance criteria.

The bottom line is that UAT testers should understand and agree on what it means to exit UAT. Your project defines the rules around what it means to exit UAT and there is no set standard or rule. The project team should define and get a consensus on the exit criteria. Here's an example for a typical software project (sample only) – the system functions correctly as proposed, all test scripts or scenarios have been executed, and the following is true:

- There are no critical defects in the core functionality.

- There are no performance issues with either critical or non-critical components. Performance issues, even to non-critical components, will be a drag on the system.

- There are workarounds for defects of high to medium importance where an immediate solution cannot be found.

In this section, we reviewed the importance of identifying the right UAT tester, engaging them early in the project to provide them with the right tools and techniques, and collaborating continuously, which results in helping us get feedback. In the next section, let's discuss what we can do to get feedback from our UAT tester about usability and functionality and why it is so critical.

Getting feedback on usability

In this section, let's explore the usability of the system. Findings around usability, such as simplification, easier navigation, and an intuitive screen flow, are not easy to uncover. We may not have a test script or test scenario for this kind of finding and, if not addressed, it may impact the usability of the system, resulting in low adoption.

By working closely with these UAT testers, you can discover these undefined, undocumented findings. I call these *findings* because they are not defects in the true sense, nor are they enhancement requests and we cannot tag them to a specific test script or even a requirement. You can call them anything, but the important thing to note here is that you have to address this for your end users. Make provisions for this kind of finding and prepare the team beforehand so that you stop bleeding valuable time during the UAT phase. If you understand why they want what they want and how it can improve the user experience, and if it makes sense, take every effort to address them.

Often, testers and business users follow a set of test scripts and continue with their testing, things work as expected, and there are flaws we will probably never find. If the business user who is testing has a deep understanding of the business logic functionality and can empathize with a broad set of end users by considering the following approaches, your end user adoption post-deployment will exceed your expectations due to the following aspects:

- A user-centric approach

- A simplified approach to navigation

- A meaningful screen flow or design approach

Let us look at a real-life example: as with other examples, this is simplified a lot and when I adopted this approach, I could figure out the flaws.

Scenario: We have a sample account plan where customers need to complete multiple tabs and complete the account plan each year. I simplified this and captured only a few fields per screen and only a few tabs so that it would be easy for you to understand and for me to drive the point across. Most of the fields on the screen are automated (as in, auto-populated based on rules) and let us assume that they can be filled in manually or auto-populated.

During our SIT phase, our QA team followed the approved test scripts and was able to complete testing without any major issues. It was the same with UAT; when the business users tested everything, it worked like a charm.

Now, let's review this screen by screen:

1. The user logs in to the system and enters the account information into the **ACCOUNT INFO** tab, as shown in *Figure 11.1*. There are required fields, some optional fields, and other automated fields. The user clicks on the **NEXT** button. Assuming the data input is good, no validation errors are visible and the user is able to successfully navigate to the next screen:

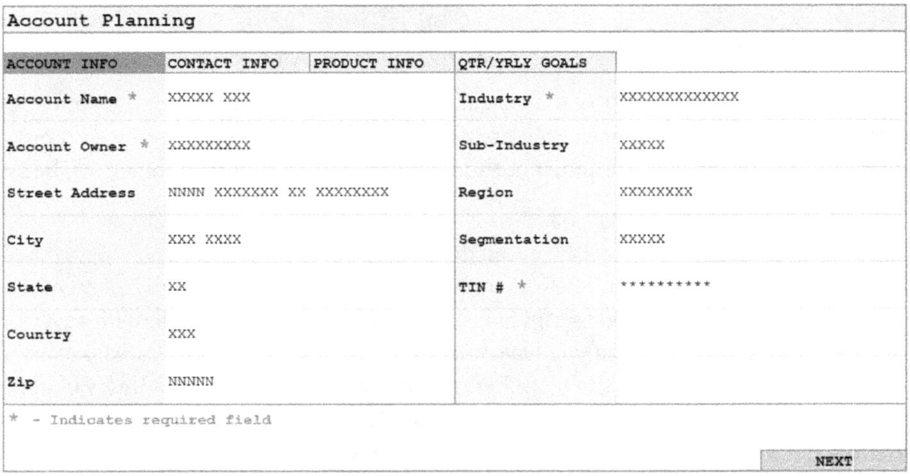

Figure 11.1 – Account Planning – the ACCOUNT INFO tab

2. The user enters the contact info and is able to navigate to the next screen. In case the user wants to go back and fix the previous screen, they have the function to go back by clicking on the **BACK** button:

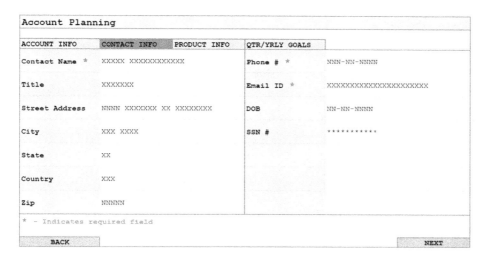

Figure 11.2 – Account Planning – the CONTACT INFO tab

3. The user enters the product info and is able to navigate to the next screen. In case the user wants to go back and fix the previous screen, they have the function to go back by clicking on the **BACK** button. So far so good and it works as per the script:

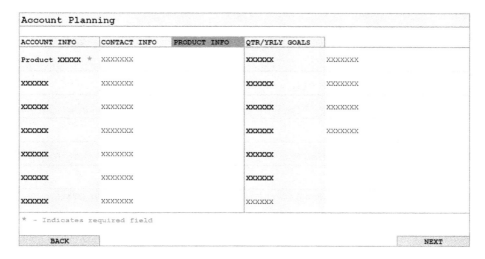

Figure 11.3 – Account Planning – the PRODUCT INFO tab

4. The user enters the quarterly and yearly info and is able to successfully submit the account plan and call it a day:

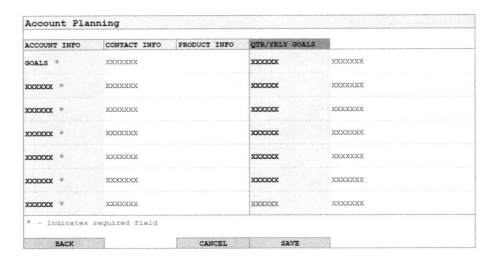

Figure 11.4 – Account Planning – the QTR/YRLY GOALS tab

Take a pause, review these screens, and see whether anything emerges from your observations. I hope you can figure out at least some of them.

Well, we can say UAT for this account planning functionality looks good and we can sign off, as the user was able to create the plan. Wrong!

Let us take a closer look together and see our findings from the business tester or super user perspective.

Our super user here is a most valuable team member and was able to point out very important features that can save the business user a lot of time, also making them a very happy user.

Let's list a few of them and this should give you the gist of what I am trying to convey in this example. Here are the flaws observed:

- The user is not able to toggle from one tab to another. In this case, if the user is on the last tab, can they go to the first tab just by selecting the tab?

- Can they save the partially completed version and save it as a draft so that it can be picked up later?

- As per the requirements, the print and email functions are enabled in the menu path (let's assume) – can we have an explicit function at the top of the screen?

- Since this is a form where the user fills multiple tabs (business plans are multiple tabs and each tab can run into multiple pages), can we change the name on the **SAVE** button to **SUBMIT**?

- Can we add a **CANCEL** option on every screen? We can go on and on in this way with hover help, an edit button, a delete button, and a clone button:

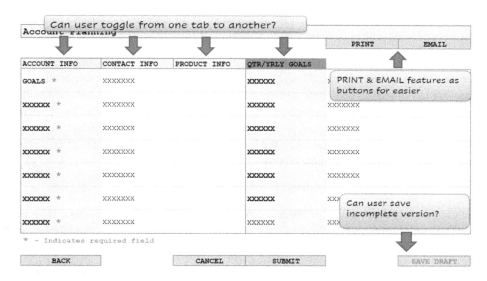

Figure 11.5 – Account Planning – overall feedback for the business user

Your team has designed and developed excellent functionality; the findings here (the flaws) are relatively trivial but make a huge difference to your end users. If we can think like our users and simplify navigation, making screen flows meaningful, we can certainly identify a few of them before the start of UAT by business users. During UAT, if we work with super users and see what they do and how they do it, it will help us deliver an excellent solution for our business users. In the next section, let's discuss the need for the UAT phase and why it is so important.

> **Note**
> This approach of testing should not take more than 2 to 4 hours for our example scenario when done by knowledgeable team members. You can see for yourself that spending a few more hours of time on this within a 4- to 6-month release will add tremendous value and make for a happy customer.

Exploring the need for UAT

We have done so many types of testing – unit testing, systems integration testing, and regression testing. Why one more type of testing? Because this is the only time the business users and the end users will be playing with a production-like system with all the functionality and data. UAT is the last available window for us to make sure that the business requirements are designed, solved, and developed to meet the proposed functional solution. It's not only the functionality but also the look and feel of the screens and the simplicity and ease of navigation for the end user for which we can get feedback.

UAT ensures that we vet out and simulate as many scenarios as possible so that the end users will not face the same issues. One critical issue on a large-scale project can impact thousands of users and this can result in wasted time, resources, and frustrated users.

So, what do we do? Do we just take the SIT scripts and SIT plan and implement the same test scripts by cloning them for UAT? See the *Testing strategy* section from *Chapter 9*, *Technical and Quality Testing*, for a recap. I have seen many projects adopting this approach and this chapter helps you understand different approaches by primarily keeping you focused on usability and the user adoption aspects of testing. Who can understand this better than the business user with all the expertise? This provides us with opportunities that can be advantageous to us.

UAT provides us with opportunities such as the following:

- Real users testing the system. Testing resources are from different business areas. They are not from IT as unit testers and SIT or regression testers are. They have business domain knowledge and they are the final recipients of the system.

- In addition to following test scripts, business users are encouraged to perform exploratory testing where testers will come up with innovative and creative scenarios that they can test. This helps us unearth issues that we never thought about earlier.

- Participants from UAT can act as a **single point-of-contact** (**SPOC**) for the end users within their business units. It helps tremendously, as other business users tend to listen to one of their colleagues from their business unit (rather than someone from the IT production support team). The SPOC can also influence the behavior of the end users and, when managed well, this can result in higher user adoption.

- Since the UAT environment is a clone of the production environment where you have all the data uploaded, this provides the testers the ability to preview their future production platform. Since we have large volumes of data, testers can run reporting metrics and dashboards, which can provide us with a general indication of how the system performs.

- It provides a great opportunity to check, verify, and validate integrations with other internal or external systems.

By the time we get to UAT, we expect that our QA team will be able to identify as many issues as possible and retest and close the majority of the identified defects. The business analyst did a smoke test and approved the environment for UAT, expecting for the most part that the system functions would perform error-free. UAT windows have a much smaller duration than SIT windows. This small window can provide us with so many opportunities and we have seen some of them. Now, let us see how these opportunities can benefit us.

Reviewing the benefits of UAT

There are several benefits to UAT. I will list a few that I found useful:

- Business users get a chance to verify and validate that the software functionality meets the business requirements. In addition to identifying defects, it helps the project get feedback and suggestions from business users. The project team can decide on whether to incorporate the requests in the same release or a future release based on impact assessment.

- This is our last and only chance to find defects before deploying to the production environment and thus reduce risk. Being knowledgeable about the testing process, they can find it fast and be able to explain how, when, why, and where they found the defect so that it can be reproduced and fixed faster. If this defect is missed during testing, it may result in different end users from different departments experiencing the same issues after deployment to production. The same issues may be described in different ways, as the end user may not be able to articulate and explain them clearly, so now in production, there may be 10 or 100 service desk tickets created with different meanings for that one missed UAT issue.

- You are able to identify the behavior of the application from the end user's point of view and ensure that usability is fine-tuned for a better user experience. This is a golden opportunity to get feedback on usability and you can solicit this from a few users. The sooner we can get this feedback during UAT, the better for us, as we plan to incorporate this feedback as much as possible into the same release. Remember that this is related to system adoption and if it were me, I would do my best to make it a great user experience.

- From a technical perspective, identifying issues – whether defect- or usability-related – can be done in a relatively short span since the UAT system is a test environment. Essentially, the project team can work hand in hand with testers and get things fixed and tested faster in the UAT environment. The same issue, if identified in production, must go through the CCB process and all the documentation and approvals and then wait for the deployment window, which can be weekly or bi-weekly.

- We can ensure the system requirements meet business needs and by the end of UAT, we can run traceability reports to make sure that at a minimum, we do not have any open defects for critical and high-priority ones. If there are any open defects, there should be a workaround and a plan to fix the issues immediately during post-deployment. UAT can help us confirm that the software solution design works as proposed and each of the software functionalities points to the system requirements and, in turn, fulfills the business needs.

Many more benefits can be identified (please revisit the *Benefits of testing* section from *Chapter 9, Technical and Quality Testing*) and I will leave that up to your imagination and creativity.

Practical tips for success

Let us look at some practical tips that may help you during your UAT phase:

- SMEs and knowledgeable users should verify that the test scenarios or scripts are valid and make sense. If the scripts are confusing or documented wrongly, such as creating the right scripts for the wrong processes, this will create unwanted defects and lead to fixing and wasting valuable time on useless defects.

- Testers should follow procedures and documentation but, at the same time, be mindful and have control over what they test. As an expert end user, if they find a test script that doesn't fit what they usually do, they need to question it so that it can be amended.

- Test core functionality before getting into secondary functionality.

- Test capabilities and functions to make sure they work before going into variants or edge cases.

- Test for high-impact functionality that may cause major issues in case of failure.

- Test things that are newly added and then test existing ones.

- Test common scenarios first in accordance with the 80:20 rule. The majority of the time, 20% of the common functionality is utilized by 80% of end users, such as creating an opportunity or a quote. So, by testing and fixing issues related to this 20%, you will result in keeping 80% of users with trouble-free functionality.

- Testers should consider broader aspects while testing – product specifications, usability, data quality, requirement problems, and supportability.

- Identify a tester who can think practically, critically, creatively, and innovatively. Challenge them to break the system.

- In addition to testing for explicit functionality, testers need to look for implicit functionality, such as usability aspects that may not be specified but make sense.

- Perform **end-to-end** (**E2E**) testing of each of your scenarios with the handover from one tester to another. As with a relay race, your marketing tester starts the process with lead creation and assignment. Your sales tester picks up the process and converts the opportunity into a quote or order, then your service tester performs the next step in the order processing. This order processing should stimulate order processing and invoice generation and appropriate notifications and data updates. The complete process should involve all the relevant systems and your UAT should touch all these touchpoints, starting with the initial data from marketing being used as starting data for your E2E test cases and ensuring that E2E data simulates real-life data processing in the system.

Time to summarize what we have learned so far.

Summary

In this chapter, we reviewed the need for formal testing and the importance of acceptance criteria to prove the real needs of our users in a production-like environment. We saw how UAT plays a key role in building the confidence of users, preparing the system for deployment, and getting ready for a rollout.

After reading this chapter, you should have a good idea of why the right UAT tester is critical for testing and how you can find the right ones and equip them with the right tools so that they can do UAT effectively and provide us with valuable feedback for addressing any problems so that we can reduce post-production issues and save time and resources.

We have completed our UAT and resolved all our concerns and now it is time to prepare for deployment to the production system. We need to keep the entire user community informed about the upcoming go-live and they need to be trained on how to use the system, as well as where they need to reach out for help. In the next chapter, we will discuss effective communication strategies, knowledge management artifacts, and other tools so that they can get acclimatized to the new software system quickly.

Questions

1. Try to recollect a few testing types that are useful during the UAT phase.
2. Name some important testing activities.

Further reading

- *User Acceptance Testing*, published by BCS, The Chartered Institute for IT

12
Communication and Knowledge Management

In the previous chapter, we discussed **user acceptance testing** (**UAT**) and why it is crucial for a successful go-live, improving user adoption and gaining trust by working with business testers. We saw the benefits from business users performing testing on real-life business end-to-end scenarios. With UAT, we saw how to ensure that the new functionality does exactly what it is intended to do and meets the business requirements.

In this chapter, we will discuss aspects of communication and knowledge management, especially focused on end users. We will not talk about project management-related communication: this we will leave to the project management team. Here, our focus is on end user communication to make sure that they are well-prepared and informed about the new software features. To be able to do that, we need to plan for end user communication and knowledge management artifacts related to the usage of the new system functions:

- Communication with our end users who will be using new features and functions related to the following:

  - Planning around training schedules

  - The availability and accessibility of knowledge artifacts

  - Support during initial go-live phases

  - Post-production support

- Knowledge management is to be planned, developed, and kept ready, specifically focused on various knowledge artifacts that are needed to enable and help users ramp up knowledge with the new functions, features, and usage of the software system.

We will discuss the following topics around communication and knowledge management:

- End user communication
- Different knowledge management types
- The accessibility of knowledge artifacts
- The benefits of communication and knowledge management
- Practical tips for success

Let's explore and see what makes for effective end user communication in the next section.

End user communication

Communication in a project is vital and the project team needs to understand that to achieve project goals, we need to ensure to do this effectively. This can be done only if we establish standard communication processes and procedures.

End user communication typically should start during the testing phase of the project. This helps provide advance notice to the end user that changes are on the way and how they benefit and help them with their job at the organization. Initial communication should be very high-level, outlining the functionality of different modules with key benefits. Periodically providing the status highlight with target dates creates excitement and interest.

I had seen many projects fail due to insufficient communication, let alone it lacking effectiveness. Thoughtful and well-planned communication based on user groups, culture, and expertise levels helps us mitigate risk. For this, we need to have a good communication strategy and implement it effectively.

Planning communication, just like all other project activities, is key. For a typical Salesforce project release, I usually consider the following important parameters:

- **Channels of communication**: Remember that one size does not fit all and it varies by organization. We need to drive the message across multiple channels until it reaches our intended audience. Let's see a few channels that I found useful:

  - **Email communication**: This is the best way to communicate with a larger audience. Drafting a simple, well-formatted email highlighting key features of the project and sending it to the group at a set frequency, such as daily or weekly, will help keep your end users updated about project information.

  - **Video clips**: A short 3- to 5-minute clip highlighting the key features and functions with software system screenshots will provide a glimpse of what's coming. This can be posted on your company website with a dedicated page for project updates.

- **Collaboration site**: From within your company network, you can use collaboration tools such as Slack, Confluence, Teams, or Chatter (or any collaboration tool at your organization) to create groups and post updates and feature functions at a regular frequency. This helps with effective collaboration through end users interacting and providing comments. When managed well, this helps adjust your communication style, as well as prepares for your end user training artifacts.

- **Posters**: These are old school, but if placed in strategic places such as break rooms, water coolers, or next to elevators, they will draw attention and curiosity. This information helps users to search for details that point to your video clips and collaboration site or the project site. If you have a TV monitor that displays company news throughout your company, see whether you can use it to showcase your project too.

- **Frequency**: Too much or too little communication is ineffective. We need the right frequency based on your audience and what works best in your context. With emails, I would say send the details weekly at the same time every week. As with video clips and collaboration sites, try to publish them at a set frequency so that you can develop a cadence for your users and make it a ritual for them. The best time to put up those posters is during the weekend (or on Monday morning before employees come into work). Anything new catches everyone's attention, and it is up to you to make that poster really enticing.

- **Identify user groups**: We need to identify and curate the knowledge artifacts based on the user base. As an example, users in the back office who use the system a lot may prefer to have knowledge artifacts documented with step-by-step instructions. User roles, such as sales analysts and service analysts, may prefer to have one-page reference sheets.

- **Communication delivery**: What I mean here is what medium do we use for communicating with end users? The business analysts or project managers can draft the communication, but it needs to go through the business sponsor or the key stakeholders. Communication should be tailored in such a way that it comes from these key people to have the maximum impact. I would also recommend the same to be forwarded to their groups by the lead stakeholder or leaders for better reach. Make sure you identify and create the groups beforehand so that it gets easier for the key person who relays the message.

- **Champions of communication**: Identify team members who are passionate about the new system and functionality and who really want this to be successful. These champions will be your conduits who can help with great user adoption. When communication comes from these champions, it is more likely that their team members will trust this person and give it a try. We need to identify and onboard them as early as possible in the project right from the elicitation of requirements. If they are one of your stakeholders, this would be even better, as they understand the progression of the business needs from end to end. These champions should be picked from respective business units and should be one to two team members from each unit. In addition, you should always use help from the project sponsor and key stakeholders from the leadership level to make communication more impactful.

- **Standardized templates**: Like all other project artifacts, these messages should be consistent and should look the same. Basically, create a brand for your project, and when someone sees the header, they should know that it is from your project.

> **Note**
>
> Create a theme for your project if it is allowed. It creates the branding for your project release. I am fortunate that this was allowed on many of my past projects. We used a logo pretty much everywhere things were related to the project and this builds team comradery and belongingness.

- **Feedback**: Communication is a two-way street. You need to listen very attentively and provide avenues for your users to provide feedback or raise concerns or suggestions. You may not be able to fix it in that release, but it will certainly help you make improvements in future releases. By being attentive, you can gain their trust and make them more attentive.

> **Note**
>
> We are not talking about change management communication. This communication is based on how to use the new software functionality and where to get help around usage.

In the next section, let's look at knowledge management types.

Different knowledge management types

In short, knowledge management is making sure the information is readily available. It can be in any form; the key takeaway is that the end users should be able to access knowledge artifacts when needed.

There are two main types of knowledge:

- **Explicit knowledge**: This knowledge can be documented and is relatively easy to obtain
- **Tacit knowledge**: This knowledge is know-how and is difficult to identify and capture

Let's discuss each in detail.

Explicit knowledge

These artifacts can be any one of the following. Based on the user base and their role, you can package a combination of relevant documents based on their job function:

- Standard operating practices
- Functional specifications
- Business process flows

- Step-by-step instructions

- Video training

- Collaborative recording tools (Webex, Teams, and Zoom)

- Cheat sheets

- Lessons learned documents

- All your project planning artifacts

- Test scripts, use cases, user stories, the RTM, and so on

- FAQ documents

Knowledge documents are living documents and need to be updated periodically to make them current and relevant. If the users are internal to the organization, it is better to provide them access to all project-related documents if it is acceptable to share as per your company guidelines. More information is good so that users can get curious and explore other areas, but at the same time, it may add confusion too. Find the right balance that you feel adds the most value in your context.

Tacit knowledge

This is the knowledge of how everyday business operates – the 5W1H (who, why, what, when, where, and how). These artifacts need to be thoroughly reviewed by your SMEs before publishing them to your users.

Let's take a look at a few good sources where we can find this tacit knowledge. Paying attention to these project artifacts and taking the time to understand them helps a lot:

- **Best practices**: These can be specific to your organization or in general to the industry.

- **Lesson learned**: The most valuable type of documentation that helps add value to your future projects by adopting what worked well and avoiding risk by avoiding or mitigating things that pose risks.

- **Problem reports/root cause analysis**: This artifact helps us with similar problems encountered in the future, which can be resolved quickly or altogether avoided.

- **Session/meetings**: Minutes from brainstorming sessions or workshops.

- **Issues/suggestions list**: These are requests originating from experts and super users who will help us with their deep knowledge, and aids us in future implementations.

- **Product support issues list and resolutions**

- **User forums**: This is where users can tell us what works well and what their pain points are. Since these are live sessions, you and the team get an opportunity to understand and elicit the needs and problems.

- **Blogs**: Business blogs help us understand the business side of the house and help us build functionality.

- **Internal communities**: Collaboration groups via Team, Chatter, and other internal group chat tools helps with great ideas and suggestions.

- **Tips and tricks**: These can be formal documents, but most of the time are discussed informally. They can be workarounds too. Make a note when you hear someone informally share these tips and tricks and document them.

Start focusing on explicit knowledge, as it is easy to create, maintain, and standardize. By having a good knowledge artifact, most user issues can be addressed easily. As for tacit knowledge, leave it to the experts in each area, who can be consulted as needed. Progressively try to document and make these available to the rest of the team.

So far, we have explored knowledge types. Next, let's see how these artifacts can be made easily accessible to our users.

Knowledge artifacts accessibility

In this section, we will discuss accessibility to knowledge artifacts and tools that you use so that your users can easily retrieve them quickly. Knowledge management deals with compiling, organizing, accessing, and circulating information. You plan, collect, compile, organize, and communicate to your users where and how to access knowledge artifacts. Let's see a few good places where we can house these artifacts. There is so much software available on the market. Use types that are relevant to your organization. I will discuss some of them that I found useful. Keep one of them centralized and sync up the artifacts to other systems, as different users may be comfortable using one or more of the systems of their choice:

- **Confluence**: Great tool and very effective if you use an agile approach to your project. This will help all your project-related documents as well as knowledge artifacts to be in one single location.

- **Salesforce**: I prefer Salesforce content management for housing artifacts and then using Chatter to disseminate links to Chatter groups. Users are able to access knowledge artifacts from the Salesforce system itself, making it more productive. Slack is another excellent collaboration tool that can be used to store and share all your knowledge artifacts.

Some sample Salesforce knowledge artifact sites are shown here:

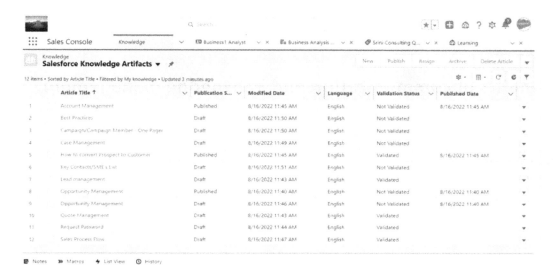

Figure 12.1 – Salesforce knowledge artifacts in Salesforce (sample)

- **SharePoint/Microsoft Teams/OneDrive**: These are other excellent tools from Microsoft. If you are using Outlook, these tools are seamlessly integrated and help with notifications and communications.

A sample Salesforce knowledge repository on OneDrive is shown here:

Figure 12.2 – Salesforce knowledge repository on OneDrive (sample)

No matter what tool you use, make sure the user can find the artifacts with ease by naming each artifact with unique and meaningful titles, keywords, and tags. This helps users find the documents in the search results effectively.

Let us look at a few benefits in the next section.

Benefits of communication and knowledge management

Effective communication ensures productive outcomes and it saves time, resources, and unnecessary frustration.

Ongoing communication with stakeholders, end users, and project team members keeps everyone aware and sets expectations. Some of the benefits are as follows:

- Reduced process time, as end users have the necessary knowledge artifacts at their disposal
- Increased productivity, as the user can now spend more time doing business and less time using technology
- Expertise gained by users
- Reduces user frustration
- Increased communication and collaboration
- Improved user adoption
- Aids in faster decision making
- Faster ramp-up (new users)

Practical tips for success

Let us look at some practical tips around communication and knowledge management to help your end user get ready for the next phase.

Here are some of the practical tips that can help you in your project implementations:

- Communicating clearly and regularly helps foster effective messaging. It provides status updates and honest assessments build confidence and trustworthiness.
- Tailor your communication with empathy, understanding, and perspective so that the recipient gets the intended communication.
- Simple, clear, crisp communication ensures that the audience gets the intended message by minimizing uncertainty, misunderstanding, and ambiguity.
- Communication enables and facilitates change. Change has to be articulated.
- Welcome feedback, address concerns, and make changes to communication.
- Information should reach those in need.

- Pick appropriate channels of communication, scope, frequency, and methods that work better for your project.

- Keep knowledge artifacts current and updated on an ongoing basis.

- You need champions who are passionate and driven and who can be the medium for effective communication.

- Follow a standard communication model or models. Use visuals as much as possible.

- Make sure the message is received by the recipient.

- Select communication methods that best fit your communication needs.

- Do not send all types of communication to everyone. Users will be drowned in the information and they may not even pay attention.

Time to conclude the chapter.

Summary

In this chapter, we reviewed the need for good end user communication and strategies around knowledge management. We need to ensure our communication is concise, clear, with a purpose, structured for coherence, comprehensive, and culturally aware. Frame your communication in such a way that the intended message is understood at the other end. Provide a channel through which the end user can reach out for further clarification.

Effective knowledge management helps lower costs and drive productivity. Investing time and resources upfront through knowledge management activities helps organizations mitigate risk by making the knowledge available when it is needed.

Managing knowledge in a central location will avoid redundancies and version mismatches. Your information can be managed in a single location and disseminated via customized links on various knowledge channels to users. This way, any changes to the artifact can be reflected at one location to keep the information fresh.

To sum up, for knowledge management to be effective, it needs to be up to date, communicated promptly, and accessible to end users.

So far, we have created excitement by communicating with the end user about the upcoming project. In the next chapter, we will cover in detail how to create great training material and short video links for user training. We will highlight the advantages of facilitating in-person or virtual training and what you should and should not cover in this training.

Questions

1. List some examples of formal communication.

2. Give some examples of informal communication.

13
End User Training

In the previous chapter, we discussed **user acceptance testing** (**UAT**) and why it is crucial for successful go-live and for improving user adoption and gaining trust by working with business testers. We saw the benefits from business users performing test real-life business end-to-end scenarios. By performing UAT, we also saw that we can ensure the new functionality does exactly what it is intended to do and meets the business requirements.

So far, we have built an excellent system of features and functions and come almost to the end, completed our UAT successfully and obtained sign off from stakeholders, and are ready for a grand go-live. The last thing left before we hand the system over to our users is end user training. What good will it be if the users do not know how the system functions, what features are available, or how to navigate the system?

End user training is as important as all other training: it plays a vital role in the successful adoption of the new functionality by your end users. Our goal here is to train our users so that they can understand the core system functionality, cross-functional integrations, and the overall process flows, connections, and functional dependencies.

In this chapter, we will discuss planning and executing effective training. Training provides us with an opportunity to help users with upcoming changes and help reduce stress. Well-planned communication and effectively delivered training, coupled with well-orchestrated post go-live super care, helps end users get comfortable with new system features.

For any activity to be successful, it needs to be planned. The project team should lay out the details of what they plan to do and how they plan to do it.

In this chapter, we will discuss the following topics around end user training:

- Planning for training
- Preparing for training
- Setting up the training environment
- Reviewing types of training materials
- Understanding the importance of in-person or live training

- Facilitating a training session

- Benefits of end user training

- Practical tips for success

Planning for training

Planning for training involves various team project team members coordinating multiple activities independently and bringing them all together before we deliver our training sessions.

We need to put together a training plan that encompasses, at a minimum, the following aspects:

- Be cognizant of our end users – who they are, where they are located, what their job function is, and how we will deliver the training.

- Identify your super users who can act as our trainers and trusted partners. It is like training the trainers, and they will be the main point of contact for their business unit and the go-to person for the users.

- Understand the scope of training – what functions and processes need to be included in the training?

- Choose the training medium – how do we plan to do the training and what methods do we adopt?

- Plan the training schedule – the dates, the duration, and the number of sessions based on user groups and user roles.

- Prepare the training material – what kind of material do we plan to provide to end users?

- Check training accessibility – how can users access training artifacts and where do we house them for ease of access?

- Review training sign-off and what it means when we say training is complete.

Let us look at a sample training schedule based on user groups:

Session ID	User Groups	Duration	Countries	MM/DD/YY	MM/DD/YY	MM/DD/YY	MM/DD/YY	MM/DD/YY	MM/DD/YY	MM/DD/YY	MM/DD/YY	MM/DD/YY	MM/DD/YY	MM/DD/YY	MM/DD/YY
CRM - 01	Sales Analyst- Session 1	2 Hrs	Asia												
CRM - 02	Sales Analyst- Session 2	2 Hrs	Asia												
CRM - 03	Service Analyst- Session 1	2 Hrs	Asia												
CRM - 04	Service Analyst- Session 2	2 Hrs	Asia												
CRM - 05	Sales Manager	2 Hrs	Asia												
CRM - 06	Service Managers	2 Hrs	Asia												
CRM - 07	Planning Division	2 Hrs	Asia												
CRM - 08	Marketing	90 Mins	Asia												
CRM - 09	Legal/Compliance	90 Mins	Asia												
CRM - 10	Production Support	90 Mins	Asia												
CRM - 11	Sales Analyst- Session 1	2 Hrs	Americas												
CRM - 12	Sales Analyst- Session 2	2 Hrs	Americas												
CRM - 13	Sales Analyst- Session 3	2 Hrs	Americas												
CRM - 14	Service Analyst- Session 1	2 Hrs	Americas												
CRM - 15	Service Analyst- Session 2	2 Hrs	Americas												
CRM - 16	Service Analyst- Session 3	2 Hrs	Americas												
CRM - 17	Sales Manager	2 Hrs	Americas												
CRM - 18	Service Managers	2 Hrs	Americas												
CRM - 19	Planning Division	2 Hrs	Americas												
CRM - 20	Marketing	90 Mins	Americas												
CRM - 21	Legal/Compliance	90 Mins	Americas												
CRM - 22	Production Support	90 Mins	Americas												

Figure 13.1 – Sample training schedule for the Asia and Americas user groups

This schedule helps users see an overall training schedule and they also can appreciate that it is not just their group but a larger part of their organization that is involved, which helps them take it seriously.

Let us look at some key features from this sample schedule:

- A unique session ID so that later, we can tag the recorded session links. It is also useful to take note of who attends which session and how many participants attend each of these sessions.

- Multiple sessions for larger groups, such as sales analysts and service analysts.

- Staggered dates so that if some team members are busy during a specific time, they can attend the other session.

- Publishing this type of training schedule beforehand gives the users advance notice. Also, say if a sales manager from Asia cannot make the session, they can plan to attend the Americas session. Later, they can review the recorded Asia session.

- Management and stakeholders get an overview of the schedule.

The next steps are to add more details and granularity of session details and time zones for each of the countries. I have simplified the following example matrix:

Americas - Training Sessions

Session ID	User Groups	Duration	Countries	Facilitator	Attendees	Time Schedule					
						US	Canada	Mexico	Brazil	Chile	Paraguay
CRM - 11	Sales Analyst- Session 1	2 Hrs	Americas	********	30	DD-MMM HH:MM AM	DD-MMM HH:MM AM	DD-MMM HH:MM AM	DD-MMM HH:MM AM	DD-MMM HH:MM AM	DD-MMM HH:MM AM
CRM - 12	Sales Analyst- Session 2	2 Hrs	Americas	********	30	DD-MMM HH:MM AM	DD-MMM HH:MM AM	DD-MMM HH:MM AM	DD-MMM HH:MM AM	DD-MMM HH:MM AM	DD-MMM HH:MM AM
CRM - 13	Sales Analyst- Session 3	2 Hrs	Americas	********	25	DD-MMM HH:MM AM	DD-MMM HH:MM AM	DD-MMM HH:MM AM	DD-MMM HH:MM AM	DD-MMM HH:MM AM	DD-MMM HH:MM AM
CRM - 14	Service Analyst- Session 1	2 Hrs	Americas	********	30	DD-MMM HH:MM AM	DD-MMM HH:MM AM	DD-MMM HH:MM AM	DD-MMM HH:MM AM	DD-MMM HH:MM AM	DD-MMM HH:MM AM
CRM - 15	Service Analyst- Session 2	2 Hrs	Americas	********	30	DD-MMM HH:MM AM	DD-MMM HH:MM AM	DD-MMM HH:MM AM	DD-MMM HH:MM AM	DD-MMM HH:MM AM	DD-MMM HH:MM AM
CRM - 16	Service Analyst- Session 3	2 Hrs	Americas	********	10	DD-MMM HH:MM AM	DD-MMM HH:MM AM	DD-MMM HH:MM AM	DD-MMM HH:MM AM	DD-MMM HH:MM AM	DD-MMM HH:MM AM
CRM - 17	Sales Manager	2 Hrs	Americas	********	20	DD-MMM HH:MM AM	DD-MMM HH:MM AM	DD-MMM HH:MM AM	DD-MMM HH:MM AM	DD-MMM HH:MM AM	DD-MMM HH:MM AM
CRM - 18	Service Managers	2 Hrs	Americas	********	10	DD-MMM HH:MM AM	DD-MMM HH:MM AM	DD-MMM HH:MM AM	DD-MMM HH:MM AM	DD-MMM HH:MM AM	DD-MMM HH:MM AM
CRM - 19	Planning Division	2 Hrs	Americas	********	5	DD-MMM HH:MM AM	DD-MMM HH:MM AM	DD-MMM HH:MM AM	DD-MMM HH:MM AM	DD-MMM HH:MM AM	DD-MMM HH:MM AM
CRM - 20	Marketing	90 Mins	Americas	********	15	DD-MMM HH:MM AM	DD-MMM HH:MM AM	DD-MMM HH:MM AM	DD-MMM HH:MM AM	DD-MMM HH:MM AM	DD-MMM HH:MM AM
CRM - 21	Legal/Compliance	90 Mins	Americas	********	12	DD-MMM HH:MM AM	DD-MMM HH:MM AM	DD-MMM HH:MM AM	DD-MMM HH:MM AM	DD-MMM HH:MM AM	DD-MMM HH:MM AM
CRM - 22	Production Support	90 Mins	Americas	********	6	DD-MMM HH:MM AM	DD-MMM HH:MM AM	DD-MMM HH:MM AM	DD-MMM HH:MM AM	DD-MMM HH:MM AM	DD-MMM HH:MM AM

Asia - Training Sessions

Session ID	User Groups	Duration	Countries	Facilitator	Attendees	Time Schedule					
						US	Japan	Singapore	India	Philippines	Vietnam
CRM - 01	Sales Analyst- Session 1	2 Hrs	Asia	xxxxxxxx	60	DD-MMM HH:MM AM	DD-MMM HH:MM AM	DD-MMM HH:MM AM	DD-MMM HH:MM AM	DD-MMM HH:MM AM	DD-MMM HH:MM AM
CRM - 02	Sales Analyst- Session 2	2 Hrs	Asia	xxxxxxxx	60	DD-MMM HH:MM AM	DD-MMM HH:MM AM	DD-MMM HH:MM AM	DD-MMM HH:MM AM	DD-MMM HH:MM AM	DD-MMM HH:MM AM
CRM - 03	Service Analyst- Session 1	2 Hrs	Asia	xxxxxxxx	50	DD-MMM HH:MM AM	DD-MMM HH:MM AM	DD-MMM HH:MM AM	DD-MMM HH:MM AM	DD-MMM HH:MM AM	DD-MMM HH:MM AM
CRM - 04	Service Analyst- Session 2	2 Hrs	Asia	xxxxxxxx	50	DD-MMM HH:MM AM	DD-MMM HH:MM AM	DD-MMM HH:MM AM	DD-MMM HH:MM AM	DD-MMM HH:MM AM	DD-MMM HH:MM AM
CRM - 05	Sales Manager	2 Hrs	Asia	xxxxxxxx	10	DD-MMM HH:MM AM	DD-MMM HH:MM AM	DD-MMM HH:MM AM	DD-MMM HH:MM AM	DD-MMM HH:MM AM	DD-MMM HH:MM AM
CRM - 06	Service Managers	2 Hrs	Asia	xxxxxxxx	6	DD-MMM HH:MM AM	DD-MMM HH:MM AM	DD-MMM HH:MM AM	DD-MMM HH:MM AM	DD-MMM HH:MM AM	DD-MMM HH:MM AM
CRM - 07	Planning Division	2 Hrs	Asia	xxxxxxxx	5	DD-MMM HH:MM AM	DD-MMM HH:MM AM	DD-MMM HH:MM AM	DD-MMM HH:MM AM	DD-MMM HH:MM AM	DD-MMM HH:MM AM
CRM - 08	Marketing	90 Mins	Asia	xxxxxxxx	12	DD-MMM HH:MM AM	DD-MMM HH:MM AM	DD-MMM HH:MM AM	DD-MMM HH:MM AM	DD-MMM HH:MM AM	DD-MMM HH:MM AM
CRM - 09	Legal/Compliance	90 Mins	Asia	xxxxxxxx	10	DD-MMM HH:MM AM	DD-MMM HH:MM AM	DD-MMM HH:MM AM	DD-MMM HH:MM AM	DD-MMM HH:MM AM	DD-MMM HH:MM AM
CRM - 10	Production Support	90 Mins	Asia	xxxxxxxx	6	DD-MMM HH:MM AM	DD-MMM HH:MM AM	DD-MMM HH:MM AM	DD-MMM HH:MM AM	DD-MMM HH:MM AM	DD-MMM HH:MM AM

Figure 13.2 – Detailed training schedules by country

If you capture the training schedule at this level, it helps you with the following:

- Scheduling more sessions based on time zones. You cannot expect users to join training sessions during off hours. This will help you plan training timings better.

- It helps you with how many sessions you need to facilitate by user group. In our example, for Americas, we have 12 sessions, whereas for Asia, we have only 10 sessions. Based on the number of attendees, we can schedule the session accordingly. In my case, I feel training may not be very effective if the number of attendees crosses 30. Based on your user base, it helps you plan how many sessions you would like to facilitate.

- This level of detail also helps us see that we are covering all countries in scope.

- It is a good artifact for your training sign-off.

Now that the training planning is successfully completed, let us start our preparation in the following section.

Preparing for training

To deliver effective training, we need to prepare all that goes into delivering the training. It takes many days and a good number of resources to prepare for the training. Let's look at some of them:

- A stable test environment for training with valid data. The system should have the latest configuration and any external apps connected to the system need to be checked off as functional (note: it may not be possible to enable all apps and interfaces working with the test environment).

- UAT should be close to complete with no critical issues. It's better if it can be done after UAT completion, but usually, projects cannot wait that long.

- Based on the grouping of users, some user groups may need more thorough training where they should be able to get hands-on.

- Collaborate with key stakeholders and leaders to encourage their teams to attend and take training sessions seriously – even better if they are mandated.

- Plan to have the training decks ready so that users can use them for reference and take notes.

- It is highly recommended that you start with relevant business process flows at a high level so that end users understand the context of the business flow and how it relates to the new functionality.

- Keep SMEs available to respond to queries.

In addition, make sure the users also have access to tools and systems during the training. As an example, if you plan to do training via WebEx or Zoom, make sure users have access to these video tools and can dial in successfully.

In all my project training, I make it a point to do the training in real time in a training environment with realistic test data. It always flows from system login to general navigation and specific functions. For me to be able to do this, I need to have a very good training environment. Let's look at what makes a good training environment.

Setting up the training environment

The training environment is very important for the trainer to provide effective training to end users. Think of the times when you are receiving or providing training and the system may not be stable or you may not have the required data or access. This affects the end user's focus and understanding of what they are learning.

These kinds of disruptions are completely avoidable and the following points will help us with this:

- The training environment is built with the latest code base and metadata.
- Trainers should create training data prior to training sessions (if needed, with the help of a business analyst).
- Each trainer should have their own set of user profiles created for their training sessions.
- Valid sample data should be preloaded when showing reports and dashboard functionality.
- Trainer access should be verified and confirmed. For example, the trainer should be able to access the system from the training location and share the screen with users.
- If users are allowed to experiment in the training environment, make sure someone is available to support them.
- Plan to provide access to connected systems and any external apps where feasible. This helps trainers to demonstrate end-to-end scenarios seamlessly. For example, by providing access to the D&B app in the training environment, we will be able to show users how to sync customer information from D&B into Salesforce.

There can be numerous other points that may be relevant to your project; the idea I am trying to convey here is that the training system has all functionalities and integrations with relevant and good-quality data. It should mirror your "to-be" production system. Before training, try to create a few end-to-end scenarios to make sure everything is properly connected and works seamlessly.

> **Note**
> Even with a good amount of preparation, some functionalities may not work. It has happened many times to me. By creating and keeping these end-to-end scenarios at hand beforehand, you will be able to show that to the users.

We have the training environment ready and have looked at the training materials that we need so that the users can follow our training. In the following section, we will look at the types of training material that we can develop. Based on the type of project, you may have to create more than one.

Reviewing types of training materials

I will keep this very brief. You do not need to be fancy to create training materials. They can be as simple as a Word document with screenshots. Let's see some common types of training materials that we all can create:

- PowerPoint or PDF deck with detailed, step-by-step instructions. This will inform and instruct the users step by step.

- Recorded training session by user role, function, or module.

- Quick reference guide. This can be a Word document or PDF file.

- Training manual for instructor-led training.

- Job aid – a simple, short, one- to two-page instruction document categorized by function, so that users can get the right information in the right format to do their job.

- Computer-based training or e-learning.

- Handouts.

We highlighted some training material types, and you can find many excellent paid training software systems that can help you with developing high-level training materials. Feel free to Google it.

> **Note**
> With the Salesforce enablement (formerly myTrailhead) site, you can publish your company-specific knowledge content on the Trailhead learning platform. It helps you deliver relevant content to the right user at the right time. In addition, from Trailhead, your user can access world-class knowledge and best practices.

In the following section, I will highlight why we need live training. In-person training is not always feasible, more so now than ever before. Let's look at and understand why it is important to facilitate and deliver live training (in-person or via web meeting) where you can interact with the end users.

Understanding the importance of in-person or live training

Many training methods can be used depending on different factors. Choosing the right method is important for training to be effective. In this section, I would like to focus on why I find in-person or live training beneficial for typical medium- to high-complexity projects and beyond. Based on the profile of your end users and project size, you can use other methods too. Let's look at some of the important factors that I find useful and use to justify conducting a live training session:

- Led by an instructor presenting to a live audience. You will be able to see the end users, share your screen with them, and interact with them.

- Users can ask questions in real time. These will be actual conversations.

- It's a good opportunity for other attendees to listen to other people's queries and interact with the trainer, as well as other team members.

- The trainer can modulate training based on user engagement. Based on the interaction and how users are engaged, the session can be managed better.

- Complex topics are easy to articulate and can be demonstrated in the training system by sharing the screen and functionality. Visually showing a real scenario in the system makes it easier to understand and helps the users point out issues if there are any.

- It can be recorded for users to replay later. Listening to the recorded session they already attended will help sync information better.

There are many other benefits of in-person or live training when done well. In the following section, let us see how to facilitate this live training session.

Facilitating a training session

Training should be tailored and facilitated as if we are telling a story with a purpose. Planning and creating the right kind of story will engage your users and you can connect with them in such a way and influence them to understand and use the system the way it is intended to be used.

In our case, when we train the users, we shall ensure that they get a holistic view of the complete business process with the functionality. In our example, it can start from logging into the system until they complete the interaction with the system. Let's see an example with the following sample steps:

- **User login**: This includes the steps for accessing the system via URL or app, resetting the password, and so on.

- **General system navigation steps**

- **Lead management**: A service analyst may not care much about lead management, but covering this topic briefly during training will help them understand the overall flow.

- **Converting leads to accounts and contacts**

- **Account and contact management**: Including integration with third-party apps.

- **Opportunity and quote management**: Integrations with other systems.

- **Case management**: A sales analyst may not care much about cases the way that a service analyst does – tailor your training to make this topic heavy for the service team and lighter for other teams.

- **Reports and analytics**: This needs to be covered for all users. Every user needs access to some form of a report based on their job function.

Each time they access the system, it should remind them of the story you told them, rather than just another training session.

For this to happen, you need to plan it early. Make sure you include the following activities or tasks during your planning activities around training:

- **Set learning objectives**: Be very clear on what you want your users to take away from your training session.

- **Develop a story**: Storytelling engages your users and, at the same time, drives the points. One size will never fit all. Tailor your story based on the user type.

- **Plan to make it interactive, encouraging questions and discussions**: Training should be interactive and users should be asking questions during the training and not waiting until the end of the session. You should not have a separate Q and A session at the end. It needs to be integral to your training and users should have an option to speak up during the session.

- **Speak with purpose**: Facilitators should understand the purpose and prepare and be very confident. Confidence is very infectious and confidence comes with good understanding, knowledge, and preparation.

- **Make your training visual**: Try to do a screen share of the system functionality as much as possible. Start with process flows to help your users understand the complete functionality at a high level before getting into more details.

- **Be prepared**: Understand the training material and the system functionality end to end completely. Go through project artifacts, training material, and the training system a few times.

- **SME availability**: Keep a few SMEs available during the training session to take any business-specific questions. It is natural that the training team may not be able to answer all queries; in such events, take it offline or get back to them later (as in, parking lot items).

- **Establish and communicate training ground rules**: For example, users need to focus without distractions, as it is not the place for discussing out-of-scope or design-related discussions.

- **Feedback**: Get feedback immediately after training. It can be as simple as 2-minute feedback around what went well and why. What needs improvement and why? Getting instant feedback is always relevant and it will help your team to fine-tune and adjust future training.

> **Note**
> Facilitate and manage your training session in such a way that makes it interactive and engaging. Apply the 80:20 rule. You get to explain the functionality and the processes 80% of the time, and your users get to ask questions 20% of the time. Encourage active participation at the same time, keeping a tab on the time spent on user interactions.

See the following sample training matrix. I use this matrix to plan my training session delivery:

Session Topics/Agenda	User Role							
	Sales Analyst	Service Analyst	Sales Manager	Service Managers	Planning Division	Marketing	Legal/Compliance	Production Support
General Navigation * Apps, Tabs, List View Controls and so on	✓	✓	✓	✓	✓	✓	✓	✓
Lead Management * Lead Functionality * Integrations with Marketing tools	✓	~	✓	~	~	✓	~	✓
Campaign Management * Campaign Functionality * Integration to third party apps	~	~	~	~	~	✓	~	✓
Account Management * Account Functionality * Integration with data enrichment tools	✓	✓	✓	✓	~	~	✓	✓
Contact Management * Contact Functionality * Integration with data enrichment tools	✓	✓	✓	✓	~	~	~	✓
Event Management * Customer Interactions	✓	~	✓	~	~	✓	~	✓
Opportunity Management * Opportunity Functionality * Opportunity Integrations	✓	~	✓	~	✓	~	~	✓
Quote Management * Quote Functionality * Quote Approval Flow	✓	~	✓	~	✓	~	~	✓
Reports/Analytics * Salesforce Reports/Dashboards * Other Analytic tools	~	~	✓	~	✓	✓	✓	✓
Case Management * Case Functionality * Case Approvals	~	✓	~	✓	~	~	✓	✓

Figure 13.3 – A sample end user training coverage matrix

The training guide contains all the functionalities and is usually common and consistent for all user groups. When delivering the training, I use the same set of end-to-end scenarios and focus on in-depth details based on the user role.

As an example, for one specific project scenario, my approach is different for each of the roles:

- For the sales analyst and sales manager roles, I go light on campaign management and case management. The focus mostly goes in depth on the details around the account, contacts, opportunities, and quote management, as this is their focus area and job function.

- Service analysts and service managers care more about the account, contacts, interaction with customers, and case management.

- Similarly, marketing users care more about leads and campaign management, and the focus of my training is more detailed based on this job function.

- When it comes to production support, I tend to cover all areas at a faster pace, as they are already conversant with different software systems.

In a nutshell, this simple matrix tells me what functions I need to cover for each of the user role groups and at what level.

Let's see some of the very common training methods:

- Individual hands-on, which is most effective but very expensive. This is usually done post production if a user runs into too many issues and the cause may be anything from network issues to understanding functionality.

- Instructor-led training for small groups where users perform tasks in a classroom setting. This is usually done for a small group of back-office users who use the system extensively to perform backend work.

- Seminar-style training where a trainer displays and walks through functionality on a live screen, demoing how to perform the tasks to users. This is my preferred style, along with many of my other colleagues at different organizations.

- Computer-based or web-based training for users to complete the training on their own.

- Training decks or guides, such as a document outlining step-by-step instructions with visual illustrations.

I found seminar-style training with a training deck or guide works very effectively. We record the seminars and provide the link to the recording and transcripts so that users can refer to the training as needed.

Benefits of end user training

Let's take a look at some key benefits of well-planned and well-executed user training:

- Effective training builds confidence among users, as training helps them see the step-by-step functionality from start to finish.

- Helps reduce postproduction queries or enquires.

- Helps users see the practical benefits of their daily activities by understanding the purpose of the functionality.

- End users get opportunities to ask questions, get clarifications, and interact with the group.

- Training helps users see that the project and business are investing time and resources. Users sense trust and feel supported.

- Job aids such as FAQs, short videos, and cheat sheets help users self-service most of the issues.

- Making comprehensive training artifacts available to users and making them available when they need it saves time for the users, as well as your support team.

Practical tips for success

Based on my experience with managing or facilitating training sessions, here are a few tips that can add value and streamline your training processes:

- Communicate clear training goals – learning objectives.

- Encourage end user feedback – pulse or valuable innovative ideas.

- To make training smooth, plan end user training early and do not leave end users for last.

- Curate training based on roles by assessing the end user needs.

- If your training budget is tight, use seminar-based training with training pre-recorded and share it with end users. You can circulate this recorded session with users and solicit for Q and A via group collaboration sites, such as Teams or Salesforce Chatter.

- Keep training artifacts current, as you may need them for retraining newly onboarded users.

- Make sure your training users get details during training on how to access the system. This includes system login URLs or desktop icons, as well as resources for resetting passwords. Also, provide useful links and contact information in case they have queries or need help.

- Make training sessions engaging, user-friendly, and interactive for them to be impactful.

- Highlight the benefits of the new system functionality and how it simplifies their work. In short, what do they gain by using the system compared to the current system or functionality?

- Create awareness of what is available and how it benefits them. This includes simple things such as list views, such as Kanban and Split View in Salesforce, creating charts from Salesforce reports, or subscribing to dashboards to be delivered via email.

- Training materials should be made available on-demand to your end users. They should be available in many forms and from many devices.

- The trainer should have the relevant skills and experience with the software application. They should exactly know what they are teaching and why they are teaching it.

- Create a short video of screen recordings (via videos and micro videos) that will help you create a visual representation of a single process – for example, how to create prospects using the D and B app or how to approve quotes. Also, make use of tools such as Salesforce app guidance or training tools that can provide users with context-based help.

We can keep adding to this list on and on. Let's end this chapter here and summarize the chapter.

Summary

In this chapter, we started with the activities and tasks to consider during planning to train your end users. Next, we reviewed the various activities that go into training preparation. Then, we discussed aspects of why we need a good training environment and various types of training materials that supplement and reinforce our training sessions. By now, you must have a good idea that live training is more impactful and how to facilitate it. We saw a few good examples and explored how they can aid us in ensuring that we covered all areas of the functionality for all our users. Finally, we concluded the chapter by understanding the benefits of training and a few takeaway practical tips that you can take into consideration for your project.

In the next chapter, which is our last one, we will cover the details on why post-go-live support is so critical and how user forms help business analysts get feedback. We will discuss in detail how regular user forums are designed in a way to help end users continuously learn about and understand the system better. Project teams can also understand pain points and get valuable insight into how to improve the system usage and thus improve user adoption.

Questions

1. List some advantages of synchronous training.
2. List some advantages of asynchronous training.

14

Post Go-Live Support / User Forums

In the previous chapter, we successfully completed our end user training. With this, we have completed all the project activities and got the go-ahead to go live with the new functionality. Our team did a phenomenal job right from understanding business requirements to developing and deploying a great solution that meets the business needs. We took our time, planned, and executed training, and made sure the team was aware of new features and functions. We also made sure that they were upskilled with all the tools and tricks on how to navigate and use the system. Finally, the day we were waiting for arrived and we implemented and deployed the new system (features and functions), which enabled access to the software system for our users.

Now, what next?

I have seen many projects celebrate and disband the project team within a week or two after going live. This is where all the problems start. For users to get adjusted to the system functionality, they need to practice a few times, and during practice, they need help and support. This is crucial for any project, and spending a few weeks during this period can help tremendously in making savvy users who can navigate the system functions with expertise. This automatically leads to excellent user adoption.

Ask yourself these key questions and you will understand why production support is critical to any project implementation:

- Do our end users know when they can start using the new system?
- How can they access the new system and its features?
- Who can they reach out to if they need help?

We will cover the following topics in this chapter to address these queries:

- Super care
- Production support

- User forums
- Delivery cadence
- Benefits of production support
- Practical tips for success

Supporting users after the go-live event consists of two parts:

- **Super care**: Short period after go-live with an enhanced support model by the project and support team. This is the stabilization period for your project and the issues can be human- and/or system-related. There is usually a super care period after every release.
- **Production and maintenance support**: Ongoing support for maintaining and managing the software system till the end of its life. Support systems are relatively stable systems where user issues and queries are addressed according to predefined and approved service-level agreements. There will be some spikes here and there, and this is the reason why we need to define SLAs.

Let's take a deep dive and explore super care in the next section.

Super care

The super care period is where you support your end users immediately after the go-live event. This is to ensure that the end users get all kinds of support in any shape or form, which enables them to perform their tasks on the newly enhanced system. The super care period usually is for 4 weeks (up to 6 weeks for very large projects) starting immediately after the go-live event.

To make super care effective, the following are some of the considerations:

- Super care should be planned well in advance as part of your project planning.
- The right resources need to be secured to support this team. This includes any cross-functional teams, **identity and access management (IAM)** teams, network teams, and so on.
- Proper communication needs to be established a few weeks before the super care starts. End users should know how, where, and who they can reach out to for help.
- Open communication channels so that your user can access real-time information and timely help.
- Facilitate at least two status meetings every day during super care, where end users and key stakeholders can dial in and discuss recurring issues and their pain points.
- Publish and communicate common recurring themes (including usability issues) and a list of known issues so that users are aware and do not report the same issues.
- Keep one person in charge of the inventory of all the issues to analyze and group common themes, so that they can be addressed as a group.

- Solve common recurring issues as soon as possible as that will cut down your call volumes drastically by almost 60-80%.

- Issues can be usability-related too; make sure that you create a simple cheat sheet and communicate to all end users the issues and steps to resolve them.

- Save all your communication-related documents and resolutions in one shared folder where everyone can view and see the status in real time. Publish status reports twice daily with ETAs for submitted issues.

- CAB members should be part of the super care and they should meet at least twice a day to review and approve or reject requests.

- Keep an eye out and understand whether it is truly an issue or a new requirement. Park all new requirements during the super care period unless it is a priority 1 issue that may be impacting a large part of the user base. You can revisit them and prioritize them once super care ends.

- Set up a video call where you can share the screen with users and, as needed, the user can share their screen with you for better understanding.

- Your user issues may not be related to the system that you implemented. It may be that your user, for some reason, may not be able to access the software system or the functionality. We need to make sure the super care team addresses and resolves the issues by collaborating with the right team and not deflecting the issue to another team.

- Involving and educating the production support team from the early phases of the project ensures that they have a complete understanding of the process, design, testing issues, and access to knowledge artifacts, including known issues with workarounds. This will help them get a good grasp of the system to be able to confidently support the application.

- Define and agree on production support SLAs. Your organization may have defined SLAs organization-wide. If not, create one and get an agreement from the stakeholders. SLAs need to be agreed on by both sides – business stakeholders and the production support leads.

- Engage super users and make sure they are fully engaged as they are the voice of the end users from their business unit and they play a key role in driving user adoption.

- Keep and document a list of recurring themes and issues. This will help you develop a strategy to resolve common issues by way of small group sessions or retraining on that specific topic.

Let us review one of the approaches. This will provide you with some guidance to get the gist of things for consideration in your projects.

For all of my projects of any size, we always ensure we have a super care period. It all depends on the size of the project, and it can vary from 1 week for simple projects to 6 weeks for complex projects. Let us consider a medium to complex project and see what we did during our super care period:

- We started our super care planning right from the project planning phase. We secured and allocated time for team members to work on super care activities, and identified the right resources skillsets, and tools required. There will be a lot of pushbacks as these activities come with a project cost and need to be planned and secured well in advance.

- We started communicating with end users about the super care agenda and what they could expect during the super care period.

- Then, we scheduled twice-daily status meetings: one in the morning and the other during the afternoon. We invited all respective super users to join this call and all users who had something to report – either an issue, clarification, or query – to hop on this call. This is the place where discussing one specific user's issue can automatically resolve other users' similar issues. All other users with no issues are welcome to join but they rarely do.

- We usually book a room called the war room and staff the room with key team members who are instrumental in resolving the issues. These resources are available during working hours (and beyond as needed). We also open a WebEx or Teams meeting for our remote users from other locations and regions to join. Team members in the office or on web calls can hop on and off as needed.

- Our team tries to understand the users' issues/queries/concerns as much as possible and we always display and share the live screen so that everyone is of the same understanding. Sometimes, we even ask end users to share their screens and show us how to reproduce the issue:

  - A simple example will prove why we need to do this. In our case, we implemented Salesforce for the EMEA region. One specific set of users had an issue accessing Salesforce and this happened only when users accessed it from that specific location. When the user was granted admin access and when our tech team logged on as the user, they were able to access it successfully. Hence, none of us could reproduce the issue even after following the right steps. So, along with a team of experts, we requested the user to share their screen so that our team could see exactly what was happening. It took about an hour and finally, one of our team members asked the user to check for the TLS protocol in their browser settings, and we found out that the user had the wrong flag checked. After checking the right flag, the end user was able to access the system. We found out from another set of users who were having the same issues. Without the ability to share screens and view and analyze the issues in real time, it would have taken forever to identify this issue.

- We publish status reports and known issues lists on collaboration sites such as Confluence or Teams so that all our end users are aware or updated with the latest news and events.

Chronologically, these are the events that take place during the six weeks of super care:

- **First and second week of super care**: During the first two weeks, we see many users having issues accessing the system or the right functionality. This could be because of the following:

- **Users do not have the right Salesforce URL, or they do not remember their password**: We can resolve this by creating a two-page document showing step-by-step instructions including how to reset the password by clicking on the **Forgot password** link. If you enable SSO, this will resolve the login issue, but they may still have an issue with what URL to access. In the case of SSO, it is always good to provide instructions on how to create a desktop icon or how to bookmark an SSO link.

- **Users with incorrect access to the Salesforce system**: There can be many factors. They may be assigned an incorrect role and/or profile. It can be related to missing permission sets, or it can be missed team members in public groups. One of the examples is that our legal team is unable to see cases for approval. When a user creates a case and submits it, cases are routed and assigned to a specific queue based on the business unit and country. As legal team members are not added to the queue, they are not able to view cases for approval/rejection.

- **Users with third-party app issues**: Many users have issues with usability when trying to access a third-party application, such as trying to sync up customer/contact data from D&B. So, we walk them through the process and create a quick two- or three-page quick reference guide for all users (we made a short video clip too). Similarly, when users try to use secondary features such as converting a prospect to a customer on account records, they need to add a KYC number and a few other details. Providing a cheat sheet will resolve issues quickly. Once users do these activities a few times, such as creating a few customer records, it becomes second nature and they do not need those reference materials anymore.

- **Users with generic queries/concerns/complaints**: We get lots of advice, suggestions, and criticism from users, and that is very common. Communicate and reinforce that this system is built for efficiency and there is some learning involved. Make a note of all those users who give both positive and negative feedback, and capture them in a document. You will find valuable information and some very good ideas that can help with future releases or enhancements. We also will get lots of enhancement requests from users forcing us to get them implemented ASAP. One of the senior team members should work with project sponsors to address them and add them to a future product backlog. At the same time, communicate the same to all the end users. This communication should come from sponsors or critical stakeholders to be impactful. We need to manage the noise and address true business user issues that are relevant to the project scope.

- **User- and system-related issues**: Any such issues, when reported, should be captured as a ticket for traceability. For the first few weeks, one of your team members or the super users should help create the service tickets.

- **Third and fourth weeks of super care**:

  - We saw more advanced secondary issues such as approval flows, opportunity and quote calculations, or issues with integrations. These need the involvement of SMEs and the technical team. Most of them take time to develop and obviously need thorough testing. We need to prioritize and then plan to deploy them accordingly based on the availability of resources.

Again, any priority 1 issues should be addressed ASAP, and for other priorities, devise a workaround and place them in your product backlog for future prioritization.

- Users will start creating and running reports and we will see issues around creating and modifying reports, report filters, report downloads, and report schedules. The same will be true for team dashboards. One common issue most often seen in Salesforce reporting is that the users are not able to see custom fields while creating reports. Make sure custom fields are added when creating custom report types. This is a very simple task, but I found team members trying to run around and wasting time trying to categorize this as an access issue.

- **Last few weeks of super care:**

  - Issues encountered before slowing down and issues related to reconciliation such as month-end or quarter-end will pop up. These are advanced issues and might be better siloed to the planning or sales operation team. You may have to work with the team and help them fix the reports, dashboards, and analytics.

  - Try to help a few users who had issues navigating the application for any reason. See whether the team can have one-on-one or small-group sessions and help them work on the system while the project SME follows them along.

  - Start requesting and enforcing users to create service tickets. Without a ticket, work should not be started, and you need to be disciplined and bold enough to enforce this.

  - Start involving your production support team and let them start handling and routing the tickets. They need to work with the project team and understand the functionality so that they get a smooth transition. They need to clearly understand that they are the ones who are going to handle these issues in a week or so.

- **Last week of super care:**

  - You should not see any more common issues. You may come across some edge case issues (the one-off scenario kind) that either your team or the production support team can handle. During this period, work on closing the super care and fully transitioning to production support with an SLA in effect. Until now, we implemented high-priority and common issues in tight small windows with approval from CAB. We did this so that end users did not lose traction and interest. This period is like an internship period, where we try to make the interns comfortable and help them navigate smoothly and understand how and where to find help when needed. Now, it is time for them to start working independently.

Now that we successfully completed super care and transitioned future tasks to the production support team, in the next section, we will look at what production support means and what makes it good production support.

Production support

Production support is an ongoing activity, and if users are using a software system, there will be issues with the system. Imagine this in the same way as maintaining your car or your central air conditioning unit. You do not know when you will run into issues, and you need someone to take care of them as soon as possible. In addition, there are preventive maintenance activities involved to keep your equipment running smoothly. This is where the production support team comes into play. There are usually three levels of production support: simple data updates and password resets are performed by level 1 support, troubleshooting user errors that can be user- or system-related and fixing minor bugs is done by level 2 support, and finally, all advanced level activities that need **root cause analysis** (**RCA**) are assigned to level 3.

The common task of a typical production support team is listed next, and I have provided a small set of examples. The list can go on and on forever.

Periodic maintenance:

- Quarterly and annual planning maintenance activities:

  - Changes to default values – as an example, the fed rates in basis point are managed as metadata and the interest rate margin field on opportunity is tied to the fed rate. Any time the fed rate is changed, the custom metadata needs to be adjusted.

  - Annual and semi-annual territory management updates and forecast management updates.

  - Updates to quote approval routing rules. For example, volume discounts vary periodically, or the level of approval may change.

- Re-org changes:

  - Many times, there may be a company re-org where you may have to make changes to data ownership, role hierarchy, sharing rules, workflows, and so on.

Bugs and issues with functionality:

- Users run into issues such as being unable to save or modify data. These are typical bugs in the code that might be there for some users. It can also relate to data.

- Some users do not have access to certain fields or records. This may be related to the fact that they changed teams and their access has not been updated accordingly.

- Users can view individual records but are not able to see reports or dashboards. This may be due to missing access to report or dashboard folders.

Data maintenance:

- Users create duplicate data resulting in skewed reports

- Users are not able to create records as the system prompts them to a dupe record that they cannot see
- Ownership changes as team members move to another department or leave the firm
- Schedule report updates
- De-dupe activities to clean up accounts and contacts

Minor enhancement requests:

- Request to add new or remove picklist values
- Request to add new fields or change field types
- Add/remove team members from workflow notification/approvals
- Request to create new report types
- Request with reports and dashboards

Release management:

- Ensure Salesforce release maintenance (three times a year) is tested and the system is error-free by the production release date.
- Also, ensure all third-party apps are compliant with their releases as well as the Salesforce release.

If the system is not periodically maintained to fulfill the business needs, it will create a lot of confusion and will impact usability and adoption. For this to be effective, we need to set some ground rules and rules of engagement. The project team needs to plan and ensure that there is a support team available so that support can go smoothly as desired. All software projects should ensure that there will be an ongoing cost of maintenance after the go-live event and budgets need to be made available to staff production support resources.

Let us see activities that can make production support effective:

- Define SLAs based on the priority that is calculated based on impact and urgency. Your organization may already have defined SLAs for all your applications. You can reuse them. The point I am trying to make is to set expectations for business users. A well-documented, agreed, and communicated SLA will keep everyone transparent.
- Staff the production support team with the right number of team members with the right skills. If you are implementing Salesforce CRM, make sure you have at least Salesforce admin-level skillset team members.
- Production support and the project team need to work hand in hand to understand and make sure there is no conflict with code and release management.

- The project team should involve production support team members with the projects and their involvement, at least from the UAT phase, will help them come up to speed.

- Business analysts should include all the production support team members during user forums.

- Project artifacts, especially the design documents and training material, should always be available to the production support team.

- The production support team should always follow the same cadence when making changes to the application (SIT > UAT > Production route). Any data loads first need to be performed in UAT and validated, verified, and approval obtained before promoting to production.

- Production support needs to look out and get involved outside Salesforce and other CRM user communities to understand the latest trends and best practices.

- The production support team can prepare the data for upload, but before uploading, the respective business users making the requests should review the final file and approve it for loading into UAT for validation. On business approval in UAT, this data can be loaded into production.

- The team should look to simplify and innovate in a way that benefits all users and not just take orders. They should say no to users if it does not add value at least to a small group.

- Set up campfires, brown bags, or other forms of knowledge-sharing sessions to educate users. This will be a good place for you to understand users' needs. This session should be more informal and educational.

- The production support team should have a weekly call with business stakeholders and provide status and walkthroughs.

- The release should always be planned and published. Here is an example:

  - Small changes, such as mass data updates or picklist additions, are done weekly every Friday at 6 PM EST (3 PM PST), excluding the last Friday of the month.

  - Any minor enhancements, such as adding new flows or Apex triggers, are done monthly at 9 PM EST (6 PM PST) on the last Friday of every month. Priority 1 releases can happen anytime with approval from CAB.

- Any system changes shall be approved by CAB, and the project SME should be one of the CAB team members.

- Always make a backup. It can be specific code such as Apex classes, triggers, or object data. In case things go wrong, you can revert. This is usually captured in your CAB artifact, but just in case it is missing from there, a backup is useful.

In addition to these activities, the production support team should be engaging super users and business SMEs for prioritizing issues. Support team members should be knowledgeable, and the project to support the transition plan needs to be well-defined and executed. This enables the support team to be operationally ready to handle and manage any production support activity. Production support leads should ensure they provide periodic status reporting and other forms of communication to all the users in scope.

> **Note**
>
> Organizations tend to provide staff production support with relative junior members assuming they are for routine tasks, and the team's job is to keep the lights on. Staff in the support team need at least one experienced, knowledgeable senior-level team member, and the rest of the support team can be junior team members.

> **Note**
>
> I recommend that all team members work on production support activities at least for a short period to really understand and get a feel for them. For junior team members, this is the place to find opportunities to learn and grow.

To make production support effective, I would like to carve out a section for user forums as I found this to be an excellent conduit for establishing rapport with the business users and being their trusted advisor. Let's look at what is involved and what made it useful to me.

User forums

The final and most important topic I will cover in this last chapter and to end the session is user forums.

User forums are periodic meetings with your SMEs, SPOCs, end users, and key production support team members to establish open and honest communication, share knowledge and understanding of their existing pain points, and get real-time feedback from the participants.

The user forum session should be about 30 to 45 minutes. These sessions are more for education and information and to be made purely voluntary. When managed well, you will see excellent participation as they are more informal in nature. These meetings give you a pulse on what the adoption would look like. This does not replace the production support status meeting and other official meetings.

Before even going into the user forums, I would like to explain why and how it helped me during my multiple implementations with many organizations to achieve high levels of user adoption. It takes some time to form and run a productive user forum.

I started this user forum to improve user adoption. Before this, we implemented multiple projects successfully and systems were adopted well for the first few months, and then it went downhill. As long as you have multiple releases, users tend to use the system well as the enhancements are rolled up into those releases and taken care of by the project teams. Once the project roadmap is completed, we need to have a proper cadence to understand the business pain points; they need at the same time to keep them aligned to the latest and greatest features to enable them to do things the efficient way.

User forums' key considerations and requirements are as follows:

- Identify one to two passionate team members from each business unit and make them the SPOC for that business unit.

- All requests are funneled through this team and prioritized along with other SPOCs from other business units during these user forums.

- Another important area is to focus on data to ensure it is current and relevant. We create many reports and dashboards to make sure key fields are maintained and dupes are eliminated. To keep data complete, we enabled workflow reminders and implemented validation rules.

- Share your users' list of development items planned to be released so that they are aware of what functionality to expect. Show them in the system and walk through them to get early feedback.

- Talk to them about the items that will be addressed in the next 2 to 4 weeks. This helps with re-prioritizing as needed and for all SPOCs to come to a common understanding and agreement.

- Take a topic and walk them through it in the system. It can be as simple as going through existing account management or quote management processes to refresh their memory on a new topic that is about to be released to create excitement.

- Discuss pain points and recurring issues that the team should be working on to address them.

- Working sessions to help team members make use of existing tools such as creating list view controls, reports, dashboards, and so on.

- Forums should be typically every 2 weeks. For a global project, you may need to divide the session into groups, and forums should be facilitated by different team members, with each team member facilitating one or two groups.

- Typical forum time should be about 30 to 45 minutes, and the business users who attend should get some value out of it. To start with, you will see only a handful of them joining. As it grows and if the business users get value, you will see larger numbers joining these forums.

- Most importantly, user forums help build trust. Trust builds confidence. Confidence builds user adoption.

- By creating a company-wide dashboard for each business unit, all users can see how their business unit is performing compared to other business units. This helps drive healthy competition.

User forums should optimally be facilitated by team members who know the business processes as well as the software system, with considerable experience facilitating meetings and workshops.

Now that you know the consideration for an effective user forum, let us look at what you should plan and cover during that short, bi-monthly session.

Topics to cover during the user forum

A typical user forum, as noted earlier, should not run for more than 30 to 45 minutes. A typical agenda for this meeting would look like this:

- Enhancements and bug fixes demo (10 mins) - features/functions planned for production deployment
- Discuss existing pain points (8 to 10 mins) - common issues faced by your users
- Knowledge session (12 to 15 mins) - pick one topic that was requested by team members
- Q&A session (10 mins)
- Two-minute feedback (ask participants what went well/where it needs improvements)
- Summary and conclusion (1 min)

End users can benefit only when action is taken. A user forum is one such avenue where you can generate opportunities to improve and enhance superior service. If you do not have user forums set up yet, you still can enhance the end user experience in the following ways:

- Periodic brown bag sessions to go over interesting topics for a wide range of users. You can invite cross-functional teams too.
- Creating collaboration groups and sharing information and knowledge tips.
- Enhance application by implementing simple automation tasks such as auto notifications, reminders, enforcing validation rules, and so on.
- Encourage active collaboration on internal and external sites.
- Deliver quick wins – easy-to-implement requests during each support release. This way, you always deliver something, and the user will see continuous delivery.
- Establish data governance, as data is the lifeblood of any organization. Spending time to keep the data pristine will help your end user and their manager with accurate metrics and reports that can aid in decision-making.
- Continuous knowledge sharing and training to your end users in one form or another to keep them up to date.

User forums provide us with a valuable exchange of information and create a good rapport with the users. To be able to deliver what is promised, we need to inform users about how the activities are planned and when they are going to be delivered. Let us see that in the next section.

Delivery cadence

Delivery cadence keeps sanity when managing expectations with your users during your production support activities. Publish delivery cadence and communicate how the requests are prioritized, scoped for production release, tested, and deployed.

Some of the key advantages of a well-planned delivery cadence are as follows:

- Establishes a predictable delivery cadence – scope of work and time duration between deliveries
- Enables better planning and cross-functional coordination
- Manages scope creeps and last-minute new work addition
- Helps balance and plan work better
- Fine-tunes and adjusts delivery cadence that fits your organization

The sample delivery cadence calendar is planned a year in advance. Again, this is planning and a few releases may be canceled due to quarter-end or year-end maintenance activities.

The following figure shows a sample delivery cadence. Publishing this kind of schedule well in advance helps manage expectations with your users.

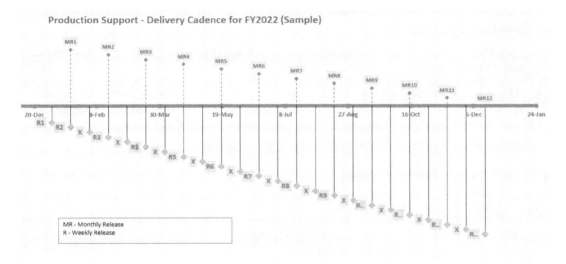

Figure 14.1 – Production support – delivery cadence for FY2022 (sample)

Let us review some key benefits of production support in the next section.

Benefits of production support

Now, let's look at some benefits that we can get from productive production support and user forums. The user forum is where we collaborate and share knowledge with business users and aids us in making production support more effective:

- Users stay current and understand the best way to use the system and accomplish their work.

- User forums provide a continuous communication channel between end users, SPOCs, and the production support teams.

- Keep everything transparent as the issues are understood and resolved based on the published SLAs.

- Users can discuss the pain point and get their requests prioritized collectively.

- Identifying SPOCs from each business unit helps team members from that business unit approach and get guidance from SPOCs, which will be more productive and effective.

- Engaging and working with business stakeholders helps keep the data clean. Good quality data helps the team with effective reporting and management with timely decision-making.

- Providing an overview of specific topics and best practices helps team members reinforce their knowledge and helps make them savvy users.

- Users and business units will be able to see many things learned from other business units based on their performance.

- User forums bring in diverse business unit users and provide a platform for discussion and understanding.

- It helps spread adoption among other business units if one SPOC or user from one business unit speaks highly of the features of specific functionality and how it benefited them with quality data. As an example, I saw the tremendous adoption of the D&B tool to enrich account and contact data when one business unit started talking highly about this tool.

Practical tips for success

Let us check some practical tips that I found useful:

- Identify the right SPOCs. They should ideally be the business users who are involved as SMEs in the project right from the planning phase.

- Staff your production support team with at least a few certified Salesforce admins/developers.

- Do not get discouraged if not many users join the user forums. Keep meeting key members and their managers individually and encourage them to attend the forums.

- Always publish the agenda beforehand. Send it a day before the session so that it works as a notification tool too. If you enabled Chatter in Salesforce, send the agenda via Chatter.

- There should be at least one takeaway and it should add value to the attendee. Ask them what topic they would like to see in the next session.

- Always sends minutes with recorded session links attached to all attendees. Keep the minutes nice and short.

- Recognize and thank team members who went above and beyond. User forums and collaboration sites are places that help spread recognition.

Let's end our last set of practical tips for success and summarize this chapter.

Summary

In this chapter, we covered details on why post go-live support is so critical and how user forums help the production support team as well as the project team get feedback. We saw the benefits of how regular user forums are designed, tailored, and facilitated in a way that meets your end user's needs helps the end user to continuously learn and understand the system better, and achieve the desired level of user adoption. A good adoption implies that we truly understood the business needs during our elicitation activity. We designed and developed the right solution, tested the system, and trained the end users well. Finally, we created and followed a sound production support plan. Production support should be planned and executed just like a project with the right set of resources, keeping it lively. Putting the right effort and securing resources upfront for production support requirements helps the production support team run the business effectively and efficiently.

Your project involves multiple sprints but your production support is one big marathon. Keep it going smoothly and steadily.

With this, we conclude our journey. So far in this book, we have covered topics from identifying requirements to supporting your end users and, in the process, giving the business users what they really need. You learned how you can add value to each of the business analysis phases by using skills, tools, methods, tips, considerations, best practices, and practical examples discussed in this book. Now it is time you put them to practical use in your business analysis work on your projects. Quickly browsing through specific chapters before you start your project phase will help you recollect and remind you of key drivers that can help you add value to your projects.

There is no right or wrong as long as you do something and try to do your best at that moment.

Keep practicing…keep perfecting….

Questions

1. What is the role of production support?
2. Name a few systems that you can use to track production support issues.
3. How many levels of production support are there?

Assessments

Chapter 1 - Identifying Requirements

1. A functional requirement describes what the software product does – that is, use case features visible to users.

    A non-functional requirement describes how the software product works – that is, quality attributes/properties that are invisible but can be observed.

2. Some of the non-functional requirements are as follows:

    *   Usability
    *   Reliability
    *   Security
    *   Performance
    *   Availability
    *   Scalability
    *   Interfaceable

Chapter 2 - Elicitation and Document Requirements

1. For a medium-complexity functionality, you do it about three times:

    *   The first round to understand current processes (automatic or manual) and high-level business needs
    *   The second round to dig deep using tools and techniques to probe further to closely understand the real needs
    *   The third round to refine your understanding and document them at a high level, review, adjust, and get consensus.

2. The most important tasks are to be able to extract and understand:

    *   **Known knowns**: These are easy to identify. Get as much detail as possible.
    *   **Known unknowns**: The users do not know these clearly; you can help get to them by using various elicitation techniques.

- **Unknown unknowns**: The users do not know what they want. They may not even know if they really want it. You can use techniques such as wireframes/prototypes to understand these unknowns.

3. If you diligently follow these tasks, you will be well prepared for effective and productive elicitation sessions:

- Prepare for the elicitation session

- Conduct elicitation

- Confirm/validate business requirements

- Communicate a summary of requirements and any assumptions

- Collaborate and make the session engaging and transparent

Chapter 3 - Prioritizing Requirements

1. Conflicting requirements are conflicting if implementing one breaks the other. So, before we can implement any, we need to resolve the conflict. For example, one requirement states, "*All service analysts shall be able to view and edit all customer cases*," and another requirement states, "*All service analysts in the planning department shall be able to only view customer cases*."

2. The major advantage is that if it is done by a knowledgeable team, you can quickly group requirements into **Must**, **Should**, **Could**, and **Would**. After you get these into the initial buckets, you can prioritize each bucket using different techniques.

   The main disadvantage is that you need knowledgeable SMEs and this technique is subjective. Some team members can wield their power and get their requirements to a higher priority.

3. Requirement prioritization helps the business get the most value for what they truly need so that they can get the benefit at the earliest stage.

Chapter 4 - Process Flows – "As-Is" versus "To-Be"

1. Some of the benefits of the current state process flow are as follows:

- You can get an awareness of the existing processes

- You can identify gaps and opportunities

- You can understand who does what and in which order

- You can identify missing, repetitive, inconsistent, and redundant steps/tasks

2. Yes. Process flows are snapshots and they keep changing as you add/remove steps in later phases of the project. What you call the "to-be" process flow will be the current state "as-is" process flow for the next phase of the project.

Chapter 5 - Business Requirements Document

1. There are four main types of requirements:

    -   Business requirements

    -   User requirements (also called stakeholder requirements)

    -   Solution requirements (functional and non-functional requirements)

    -   Transition requirements

2. Transition requirements are important as they ensure business continuity and are very critical for a project's success. Examples include data conversions and end user training requirements.

    Think of a scenario where you are migrating from a legacy system to a new cloud-based system; you need to plan to migrate legacy data to the cloud. This migrated data should be usable, and users should be able to create and complete transactions effectively.

3. Past project documents such as BRDs, **Functional Specification Documents** (FSDs), and test scripts/scenarios. The majority of the non-functional requirements can be identified from these artifacts. If your implementation is brand new, refer to best practices or blogs in user communities.

Chapter 6 - Solution Design and Functional Document

1. The following are a few benefits of a good functional document:

    -   Helps you understand the features to be developed/tested

    -   Provides a clear scope

    -   Streamlines the development process

    -   Aids in planning and documenting test scripts

2. The following are the three artifacts you may find useful during the solution design phase:

    -   Conceptual flow

    -   Architectural flow

    -   Process flows

3. The following three key participants are required during the solution design phase in addition to you, as a business analyst:

    -   Solution/technical architect

    -   Technical lead/manager

    -   Project manager

Chapter 7 - Demonstrate Functionality Using Prototypes

1. A prototype is used to demonstrate or test chunks of functionality incrementally whereas piloting is operational functionality delivered to a small set of users. If approved, this pilot functionality can be implemented for larger groups.

2. Horizontal prototyping is useful during high-level requirement gathering – for example, the business requirements phase, where all system functions are defined or designed at a high level.

    Vertical prototyping is useful during detailed requirements gathering – for example, in a functional design document where we need to capture an entire set of tasks for a function that includes functional and non-functional requirement details.

3. Some of the prototyping techniques include the following:

    *   Throwaway
    *   Evolutionary
    *   Operational
    *   Incremental
    *   Horizontal
    *   Vertical
    *   Rapid or dynamic system development

Chapter 8 - Exploring Conference Room Pilots

1. CRPs provide many benefits. Some of them are as follows:

    *   Confirm and validate the understanding of business needs
    *   Early feedback
    *   Opportunities for improvement of the overall solution
    *   Innovative ideas and solutions

2. Change control, also referred to as the **Change Control Board** (**CCB**), helps manage the scope by approving or rejecting changes to the project/system.

3. When there are resource constraints, you can optimize CRP by ensuring high-impact requirements are given the highest priority.

Chapter 9 - Technical and Quality Testing

1. Here are some automated testing tools:

    - Selenium

    - HPE Micro Focus UFT

    - HPL Software

    - Provar

    - Ranorex

    - TestingWhiz

    - Sahi

    - Waitir

2. These two are completely different. Re-testing deals with test cases that failed earlier during testing and after fixing. Regression testing is done on passed test cases and is for entire functionality to be checked for unexpected side effects, aiming for no additional problems to be introduced.

3. User acceptance testing, regression testing, and system testing are some examples of blackbox testing. This method of testing lets the user test functionality of the software without the ability to see the internal details such as how it was coded.

Chapter 10 - Requirements Traceability Matrix

1. Forward traceability helps us to ensure that we are building the solution/functionality correctly.

2. Backward traceability ensures that we are building the right solution/functionality. It traces back from test case -> test script -> design spec -> functional spec -> process flows -> business requirement.

3. True

4. True

Chapter 11 - User Acceptance Testing

1. Some of the types of UAT are as follows:

    - Alpha testing

    - Beta testing

    - Black-box testing

    - Operational testing

2. The following are key activities:

- Planning

- Configuring

- Operating

- Observing

- Evaluating

Chapter 12 - Communication and Knowledge Management

1. Examples of formal communications are as follows:

- Presentations

- Agendas

- Meeting minutes

- Status reports

2. Examples of informal communication are as follows:

- Chats

- Social media

- Emails

- Side conversations

Chapter 13 - End User Training

1. Some advantages of synchronous training are as follows:

- Real-time interactions

- Questions are clarified immediately

- Helps modulate session delivery

- Individual attention for those needing extra help

2. Some advantages of asynchronous training are as follows:

    -   Anytime, anywhere

    -   Ability to revisit content

    -   Easy to deliver

Chapter 14 - Post Go-Live Support / User Forums

1. The primary role of production support is to make sure the systems are running efficiently, and that users can use the system effectively.

2. Some of the production support tools are ServiceNow, Jira, Remedy, and Wrike. You can use a simple spreadsheet too!

3. There are three levels:

    -   Level 1: Password resets and simple data updates

    -   Level 2: Troubleshooting errors and fixing minor bugs

    -   Level 3: Advanced-level troubleshooting and root cause analysis (RCA)

Index

Packt.com

Subscribe to our online digital library for full access to over 7,000 books and videos, as well as industry leading tools to help you plan your personal development and advance your career. For more information, please visit our website.

Why subscribe?

- Spend less time learning and more time coding with practical eBooks and Videos from over 4,000 industry professionals

- Improve your learning with Skill Plans built especially for you

- Get a free eBook or video every month

- Fully searchable for easy access to vital information

- Copy and paste, print, and bookmark content

Did you know that Packt offers eBook versions of every book published, with PDF and ePub files available? You can upgrade to the eBook version at packt.com and as a print book customer, you are entitled to a discount on the eBook copy. Get in touch with us at customercare@packtpub.com for more details.

At www.packt.com, you can also read a collection of free technical articles, sign up for a range of free newsletters, and receive exclusive discounts and offers on Packt books and eBooks.

Other Books You May Enjoy

If you enjoyed this book, you may be interested in these other books by Packt:

Becoming a Salesforce Certified Technical Architect

Tameem Bahri

ISBN: 9781800568754

- Explore data lifecycle management and apply it effectively in the Salesforce ecosystem
- Design appropriate enterprise integration interfaces to build your connected solution
- Understand the essential concepts of identity and access management
- Develop scalable Salesforce data and system architecture
- Design the project environment and release strategy for your solution
- Articulate the benefits, limitations, and design considerations relating to your solution
- Discover tips, tricks, and strategies to prepare for the Salesforce CTA review board exam

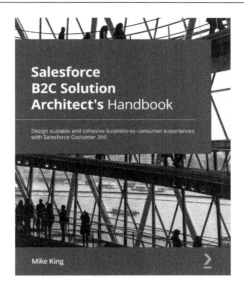

Salesforce B2C Solution Architect's Handbook

Mike King

ISBN: 9781801817035

- Explore key Customer 360 products and their integration options
- Choose the optimum integration architecture to unify data and experiences
- Architect a single view of the customer to support service, marketing, and commerce
- Plan for critical requirements, design decisions, and implementation sequences to avoid sub-optimal solutions
- Integrate Customer 360 solutions into a single-source-of-truth solution such as a master data model
- Support business needs that require functionality from more than one component by orchestrating data and user flows

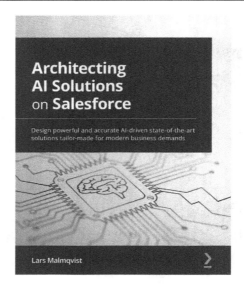

Architecting AI Solutions on Salesforce

Lars Malmqvist

ISBN: 9781801076012

- Explore the Salesforce's AI components and the architectural model for Salesforce Einstein
- Extend the out-of-the-box features using Einstein Services on major Salesforce clouds
- Use Einstein declarative features to create your custom solutions with the right approach
- Design AI solutions on marketing, commerce, and industry clouds
- Use Salesforce Einstein Platform Services APIs to create custom AI solutions
- Integrate third-party AI services such as Microsoft Cognitive Services and Amazon SageMaker into Salesforce

Packt is searching for authors like you

If you're interested in becoming an author for Packt, please visit `authors.packtpub.com` and apply today. We have worked with thousands of developers and tech professionals, just like you, to help them share their insight with the global tech community. You can make a general application, apply for a specific hot topic that we are recruiting an author for, or submit your own idea.

Share Your Thoughts

Now you've finished *The Salesforce Business Analyst Handbook*, we'd love to hear your thoughts! Scan the QR code below to go straight to the Amazon review page for this book and share your feedback or leave a review on the site that you purchased it from.

`https://packt.link/r/1-801-81342-6`

Your review is important to us and the tech community and will help us make sure we're delivering excellent quality content.

Download a free PDF copy of this book

Thanks for purchasing this book!

Do you like to read on the go but are unable to carry your print books everywhere? Is your eBook purchase not compatible with the device of your choice?

Don't worry, now with every Packt book you get a DRM-free PDF version of that book at no cost.

Read anywhere, any place, on any device. Search, copy, and paste code from your favorite technical books directly into your application.

The perks don't stop there, you can get exclusive access to discounts, newsletters, and great free content in your inbox daily

Follow these simple steps to get the benefits:

1. Scan the QR code or visit the link below

https://packt.link/free-ebook/9781801813426

2. Submit your proof of purchase

3. That's it! We'll send your free PDF and other benefits to your email directly

www.ingramcontent.com/pod-product-compliance
Lightning Source LLC
Chambersburg PA
CBHW060550060326
40690CB00017B/3663